FROM THE Jungle TO THE Boardroom

From the Jungle to the Boardroom

Copyright © 2011 by ThinkMonahan, LLC

Jacket design by Michael R. Mitzel
Book interior design by Jaad Book Design
Book edited by Ann Weber
Author photo by Julie Monahan Hogan

FROM THE Jungle TO THE Boardroom

MIKE MONAHAN

To Michelle
Lots of Luck,
Mike

Beacon
PUBLISHING

This book is dedicated to...

The leaders who hold on against all odds
and make their dreams come true.
My champions who assisted me in
making this project a success.

Mike and Chico in Vietnam, 1969.

TABLE OF CONTENTS

The Day My Life Changed

As our jet touched down and the captain turned off the air conditioning, I immediately felt the heat. An indescribable odor seeped into the plane.

The door of the plane opened as the engines went silent, and a set of stairs was pushed in place. As I stepped through the door, the heat almost knocked me over. It actually took my breath away.

I was filled with fear and, with each step, I could feel the fear taking over. It seemed like there were a hundred steps, but I finally came to the last stair. My life was about to change forever.

I took that final step onto the tarmac. I'd just entered a world that I'd dreaded for so long.

It was May 14, 1969. I was in Vietnam.

To my surprise, I heard applause. I saw a hundred or so men in worn-out fatigues. They looked exhausted. They were clapping, which seemed strange.

But then it hit me why they were clapping. The ovation wasn't for us. They were applauding the *seats* in which we'd just arrived. They were excited because in a few minutes, after the plane refueled, they would board the jet to fly back to "the world," back to the United States. They had made it through their Vietnam tour.

Mine was just beginning.

As we walked toward the check-in area, I felt sick to my stomach. I walked by all the GIs waiting to go home. They were weathered and worn out; I could see it in their faces. I tried to imagine me standing there a year later, but I couldn't. It just didn't seem possible.

The other arriving soldiers and I went into a makeshift wooden building with a tin roof. As I waited to be helped, I could hear the plane engines rev. A few minutes later, the jet took off, beginning the trip home.

I couldn't believe that I really was in Vietnam.

It seemed like it took forever to process our information. I just wanted to get to where I was going so I could figure out what I needed to do to get my head straight.

For the next few days, I was close enough to Bien Hoa Air Base to see planes come and go. Twice a day, flights would arrive from the US, delivering new troops and then returning soldiers home from the war. As I watched each flight leave, I had a sinking feeling in my gut. All I could think was, *I will never make it home! The odds are slim to none that I can make it home in a year.*

I was depressed. This was my worst nightmare. I was twenty years old, away from home, in a foreign land.

I really was in Vietnam.

Each day as I watched the planes leave for "the world," I became more depressed. One day as I stood watching, I knew that I somehow needed to change my attitude. But at that moment, I didn't know how I would get over my feeling of hopelessness.

How could I convince myself that I could make it through alive and be on a plane heading back home in a year?

My Story

It's been more than forty years since I returned from Vietnam, but I can still remember certain things like they happened yesterday. I was twenty years old when I arrived in Vietnam. One year later, when I returned home, I felt much older than twenty-one.

Oddly enough, returning home from the war wasn't as easy as it would seem. Americans were tired of seeing the killing on the news, and it was reflected in the country's mood. The feeling was, "Let's not talk about it!" So I didn't talk about it. That worked out pretty well, because I didn't know what I wanted to say about my year in Vietnam, anyway. I had feelings stuck inside me, and I really wasn't sure what they were about.

When I was sent to Vietnam, I was told that I'd be fighting for freedom. Maybe it was just me, but I spent a full year in Vietnam and never once did I feel like I was fighting for freedom. I never felt like the Vietnamese people saw us as fighting for their freedom, either. We simply patrolled and never took control of anything.

I was actually in a fight for my life.

I'm still not sure what the whole war was about, and I never will be. I probably wouldn't believe the truth even if I heard it today, because I have too many of my own opinions.

My memories of my time in Vietnam and the stories I'm sharing with you are both comical and serious, and I'll show you how they relate to everyday situations—at work and at home. But my stories aren't tragic, like many depictions of the war in books and movies.

So I have a few fears about sharing my story with you. First, I feel as if I was lucky and that I may offend the real heroes of the war by telling my story.

My second fear is the same fear I had when I came home in April 1970, and that's the fear of being ridiculed.

I'm proud that I served in Vietnam but hate the fact that we never seem to learn from our mistakes. The thought of my wife, Nancy, and I sending one of our children or grandchildren to war makes me feel sick.

In the following pages, I'll share three questions that I asked myself while I was in Vietnam. And I still ask myself these three questions each day—as a husband, dad, and executive director/CEO of a non-profit organization:

1. Am I prepared?
2. Am I safe?
3. Am I alone?

These are leadership questions. We're all leaders, twenty-four hours a day—we're leading ourselves and we're leading others at work and at home.

The three questions seem pretty simple, but they aren't easy. And you may be surprised by my answers!

Am I Prepared?

Am I prepared? Am I safe? Am I alone?

What does the concept "prepared" mean to you? Does it mean that you have all the answers? Or does it mean that you are willing to take a risk?

Defining what "prepared" means to you will be critical to your future success.

If you need all the answers before you move forward, you might miss many opportunities. If you're prepared to take risks, your outcomes surely will be different.

Think about it. How many times do you ask yourself the question, "Am I prepared?" in some form? When your boss has a new project and wants you to lead the team, does the question come up? When you and the person you're dating wonder if you should get married and have a family, does the question cross your mind?

How will you know that you're prepared?

When I was drafted into the Army and sent to Vietnam nine months later, I was told that I was prepared.

I didn't feel that way.

You really won't know how prepared you are until you finish what you're attempting. I asked the question when I decided to have children back in 1970, and I'm still asking the question today!

The question, "Am I prepared?" sounds a little different now because my kids are grown and have their own children, but I'm still their dad. I feel better prepared than I did forty years ago, but the issues are different and the challenges are new.

When you think about life, we all spend an enormous amount of time in the "prepare" mode. It's easy to put off what you really want because you don't think that you're prepared to do it perfectly. I see people put great ideas on hold and eventually just give up. Why? They don't think that they're prepared, and they don't want to risk failing. So they don't do anything new.

In areas of risk, we often feel as if we're not prepared. Do you avoid moving forward when you feel that you aren't completely prepared?

We also spend enormous amounts of time in the "repair" mode. In life, something always needs repair. Something always has to be done. Something always demands our attention. It's easier to do what is familiar than to do the things that require risk. Many people never go anywhere or do anything because something else was more important.

The question about preparedness that we all have to ask is, "Do I trust myself?" I love the idea of preparation, but there's no guarantee that the outcome will match the preparation.

Trust, on the other hand, is about the moment you're in. If you trust yourself, you'll continue to adjust your ideas. If you trust yourself and are committed to the final result, it's hard not to end up where you intended to be. In an odd way, that *is* preparation!

When life changes, no one will ask you, "Are you prepared?"

The Draft

graduated from high school in spring 1967, and the draft for the Vietnam War was in high gear. At that time, you could get a student deferment if you went to college. That was a good thing for anyone who wanted to avoid the draft. As you can imagine, the demand for higher education was considerable!

School had been a painful experience for me, and I had no intention of going on to college. The only vision I had for my future was to hang out and wait to be drafted. I figured that it was just a matter of time until I was called into the Army. I lived at my parents' home in Cincinnati, so I didn't need much money. I worked odd jobs.

In May 1968, a good friend approached me with an idea. Tim wanted to know if I'd join the Marines with him on the "buddy plan." He said if we joined together, the Marines guaranteed that we'd be stationed together.

As much as I liked Tim, I didn't like his idea very much. The Marine Corps had a reputation of having the toughest training of all the services, and I wasn't a very tough guy. All hell was breaking loose in Vietnam, and the Marines seemed to be front-and-center in the war. The pictures on the nightly news were graphic, and they were usually of Marines being killed and injured.

I told Tim he was crazy—enlisting was almost a 100 percent guarantee that he'd go straight to Vietnam after completing basic training. We talked a lot about it, and Tim told me that his dad was a Marine. Tim wanted to follow in his father's footsteps.

While I understood how Tim felt, I had a different view of being a Marine. Tim came from a healthy family, and his dad was a great role model. Tim wanted to make his dad proud and uphold the Marine Corps tradition. My dad wasn't a great role model or a veteran, so I had nothing to prove or any tradition to uphold.

The honest answer? I decided that my odds of *not* going to Vietnam were better if I waited to see if I was drafted. I was nineteen. I didn't feel prepared at all to face war. Besides, the Army seemed to have more safe places, like Germany, where I could be sent to serve. Tim ultimately decided that he would go ahead and join the Marines without me, and he soon enlisted for two years of active duty in the Marine Corps.

I chose to wait and see what happened, not only to gain time but also because I really didn't like making decisions. "Wait and see" was my typical way of operating. I didn't have to wait very long before I saw!

I received my draft notice to report for my physical in July. I passed with flying colors. I was ordered to report for active duty in thirty days. I was about to discover that the Army was more than happy to make all my decisions for me.

They were prepared to take total control, whether I liked it or not.

Not Doing Anything Is Doing Something

When I was nineteen years old, I didn't realize that to *not* make a decision is actually making a decision. By not making a decision about the military, I agreed to leave my future to chance. I let the outside world decide for me.

My buddy Tim made a decision to take charge of the military options he faced. While he didn't have total control of the outcome, he chose to have input. Tim decided to act, and I decided to wait and leave my life to chance.

After Vietnam, I could see many situations in which my behavior followed this do-nothing pattern. When I returned home, I married the woman I had dated before leaving for Vietnam. We eventually had four children—two girls and two boys. The marriage was a struggle, even from the beginning.

We had little hope of success because we weren't prepared to cope with the events that life presented. Many of our problems were the classic contributors to many a failed marriage: lack of money, drinking (me), babies to care for. You name it, we had it going on.

The marriage ended after fourteen years, when I decided that I wanted a divorce. I was unhappy in the relationship and couldn't see any resolution. My life was beginning to seem hopeless.

At that time, it was pretty uncommon for a father to have custody of the children. While I didn't feel that I was prepared to take charge, I felt I needed to. My children were ages fourteen, thirteen, eleven, and three. It was quite scary and challenging for me to be a single parent.

It doesn't matter what you do or where you are in life, you face the dilemma of making decisions each and every day. You have a choice, and you can make the decisions or leave your life to chance. Remember, you won't really know if you're prepared for what you're doing until you've done it.

In my first marriage, I put off for years my decision to divorce. I knew the marriage wasn't working, but I didn't want to be the bad guy in the eyes of the people around me. I thought I would be judged and blamed. I knew what to do, but I used excuses so I didn't have to do anything. I wasn't ready to face the consequences of my actions.

Because I didn't have the courage to make the decision, everyone (me, my ex-wife, our four kids) paid a price.

People often want to avoid conflict so they defer making decisions, such as I did with the draft and getting divorced. In what areas are you leaving life to chance because you don't feel prepared to make a decision?

In your relationships, do you keep quiet during disagreements because you don't want to rock the boat? Maybe an underperforming employee affects your whole team at work, but you don't hold them accountable. Or it could be as simple as avoiding yearly medical examinations that may catch a health problem before it become too serious to treat.

In so many areas, we put decision-making on hold and leave life to chance.

If you want to take action, you first have to acknowledge what you're avoiding. Remember: To *not* make a decision is to make a decision! It's critical for you to develop your decision-making skills.

We're all leading someone. When you think you're not prepared and you hesitate to make a decision, you leave your future to chance—the future of your family, the future of your career and the future of the people who follow you.

Hesitation is a decision—a time that can never be recaptured.

Basic Training and a Whole New World

On August 15, 1968, I boarded a bus headed for Fort Benning, Georgia, and basic infantry training. I was about to enter a whole new world that would change the course of my life.

I will never forget the sick feeling I had as I left the home I knew. The bus ride seemed to last forever, and I don't recall speaking with anyone the entire trip. I'd never been away from home before, so it was hard for me to grasp that I was leaving for two years.

It was absolutely crazy when we finally arrived at Fort Benning and stepped off the bus. Drill sergeants screamed in our faces: "Run here!" "Run there!" It was totally nuts. Those in command seemed to get great pleasure from yelling at everyone.

It was early evening, and everyone was tired from the long bus ride. I remember a few guys making jokes and, within two minutes, it was clear to me that humor wasn't going to cut it in the Army.

Screaming and confusion—and these were only my first few minutes in the Army! I knew this was going to be the most difficult experience of my life so far. It wasn't going to be anything like living at my parents' house and working part-time.

Basic infantry training was designed to break us down, get us in shape, and teach us to take orders. It was all about humiliation and breaking the individual spirit.

The training process quickly moves the trainees from being an individual to the "you-and-your-buddies-are-one" concept. If one person screws up, everyone pays the price. In the beginning, we all looked out for each other, but everyone moved amazingly quickly to the mob mentality in order to avoid punishment.

I vividly remember an example of this. When we ran—which was all the time—we ran in formation and sang songs to keep pace. A guy in my platoon was heavy and had a hard time keeping up with the rest of us. In the beginning, guys in the platoon would take turns helping him by carrying his gear or putting a shoulder under his arms to move him along. Everyone felt sorry for him and wanted to help him.

We quickly learned we would all pay a price for his quitting, so no one wanted him to fall out of formation. It only took a few days for the help to turn into threats and aggressive behavior. People kicked him and told him that if he stopped running, he would get his ass kicked back at the barracks later in the evening.

This type of pressure took place all the time, and you never knew whom you could trust and whom you couldn't. Tension was everywhere, and I found myself looking over my shoulder for the next unexpected challenge.

The physical, mental, and emotional challenges often were more than I thought I could handle. I wasn't prepared, and I felt as if I was thrown into a completely different world.

I quickly realized that I'd lived a sheltered life. For the first time, I faced the differences between people who grew up in the North and the South. I witnessed prejudice like I'd never seen before in my white neighborhood. What really blew me away was religious prejudice. Before basic training, I didn't even know that it existed.

I didn't trust anyone.

Basic training lasted for three months, and we learned about everything from handguns to artillery. We learned how to read maps, shoot different weapons, and navigate with the use of a compass. We learned how to take orders without asking questions. We learned how to be mentally prepared to survive, no matter what happened.

One day, a drill sergeant was in my face, and I felt something in me snap. In that moment, I was glad that I didn't have a loaded weapon.

I wanted to kill him. That was the only time in my life that I ever experienced that feeling.

In the end, he did his job. He broke me.

Basic training was painful. As I said earlier, basic training was all about physical, mental, and emotional conditioning. I saw guys go off the deep end. I saw men go AWOL (absent without leave) and end up classified as deserters. I saw good guys who were humiliated and driven to the edge.

It seemed like basic training lasted for an eternity, and yet, at the same time, I really didn't want it to end because I knew that when it did, I likely would be one step closer to Vietnam.

After ninety days, basic training did finally end. While we had been constantly busy at Fort Benning, I sure didn't feel as if I was prepared to fight a war.

Do you remember my friend Tim? I thought he made a stupid decision to join the Marines, which increased his odds of going to Vietnam. While I was in basic training, I received a letter from Tim. He'd successfully completed Marine Corps basic training, and was headed to Twentynine Palms, California, for the next one-and-a-half years, where he would finish his active duty with the Marines. Tim was going to be safe and sound in the US for his military duty.

So much for my wait-and-see attitude and my ability to accurately predict the future!

Peer Pressure

When people talk about peer pressure, they usually associate it with children, especially teenagers. Teenagers are so impressionable and want to fit in.

But if we take the time to look at peer pressure, don't we all face that kind of stress, whatever our age? Have you ever been in a work environment filled with negativity? Maybe someone criticizes people behind their backs. In the beginning, you stay out of the gossip. But just like my experience in basic training, the group can wear you down, and, before you know it, you've joined the mob scene.

If you're not prepared to stand for your own values, you'll always default to the group that surrounds you.

After my divorce, a woman was interested in me, but I had trouble believing it. Nancy was in charge of the credit union I belonged to. And the reason I thought she wouldn't be interested in me? She was thirteen years younger.

Well, Nancy really was interested, and so was I. We dated and became serious very quickly. Nancy had a son who was two years old, and I had my four kids, who now ranged from ages three to fifteen. Both of our families were very concerned that we'd gone off the deep end. Her family worried that she was serious about an older man with four kids. My family thought I was robbing the cradle.

Nancy and I decided that we were prepared to face the challenges that marriage would bring our way. When we decided to marry, pressure came from both sides. Prenuptial agreement, wills, you name it. Our families pushed both of us to reconsider.

Maybe you wouldn't call it peer pressure, but I would; they put pressure on us to do what they thought we should do.

When you're not sure of yourself, outside pressure can take over and lead to you following others. There's nothing wrong with following and being influenced, but it's important that you know whom to follow! When you're clear and focused, *you* are the influencer and the leader.

The longer you stay in an environment that lacks your values—the longer you live your life for others—the more stress you'll experience. Many people work for companies that don't fit their value system. They think that the paycheck makes it okay. If one employee is out of alignment, the whole team suffers. Just like the guy in my platoon who couldn't keep up, everyone has to carry the person who isn't really part of the team. And everyone will resent that person.

We are affected by the environment or culture where we spend time. This is a form of peer pressure.

Are you prepared to take it?

If you live your life for others, you'll need a larger casket so you can bury your dreams with you.

AIT, aka Basic Training All Over Again

My next stop after basic training was Cincinnati. I had a short leave to see my family and friends. After my visit home, I reported to Fort McClellan, Alabama, for advanced infantry training (AIT).

AIT lasted ninety days and was a rerun of the same attitudes and tactics I experienced in basic training. Once again, the drill sergeants' primary job seemed to be messing with our minds while preparing us for the inevitable tour in Vietnam.

It's been so many years, it's hard to determine the accuracy of my thoughts about my experiences. But the approach I remember them using to "lead" us seemed juvenile. It didn't feel like adult leadership. Just like basic training, AIT was a mind game designed to break our will and make us follow orders.

I remember what the drill sergeants called "fire drills." Fire safety wasn't involved. We had to move the entire contents of our barracks outside. We'd then clean and wax the entire barracks, which would be followed by an inspection. Next, we were instructed to return all of our belongings to the barracks. All of this had to be done very quickly.

Once we had everything inside, we had another inspection. As you can imagine, we would—of course—mess up the floors when we brought the beds and footlockers back inside. So we failed the inspection and had to do the entire routine again. The end result of this exercise was that we carried everything in and out, plus cleaned the barracks, several times. But the larger point was to let us know that we were at the mercy of the drill sergeants.

The purpose of AIT was to prepare us to be soldiers by teaching us more about combat situations and further training us on using weapons. We spent a lot of time learning how to fire and take care of our weapons. We now better understood all of the weapons used by the Army in Vietnam, especially the M16 rifle. It was stressed over and over again that when we reached Vietnam, taking care of your M16 could be the difference between life and death.

In AIT, we prepared for war by training in simulated Vietnamese settings. We patrolled as if we were in Vietnam, on an actual mission. We learned about the perils of walking down a footpath, and how many traps were set to injure soldiers, including tripwires, pits, and booby-trapped "souvenirs," such as a Vietnamese flag or pistol left on the trail for curious American soldiers to pick up. They taught us how to secure a village, even when we couldn't tell the enemy from the civilians. We also had to navigate a course with a compass while avoiding enemy troops; this course included a torture tent if you were caught.

At twenty years old, it was rather difficult for me to imagine how this training related to my tour in Vietnam. What were the odds, after being pulled out of the life I knew, that 180 days of training had prepared me to kill someone? I'd shot my brother's pellet gun a few times. I'd been in one fight in my life, and I lost. When qualifying at the rifle range in basic training, I passed, but at the lowest possible score. I told everyone that when I got to Vietnam, I would keep my M16 on automatic because that was the only way I would hit something!

I was hardly prepared for war.

But AIT was about to end, and, with just six months of training, most everyone would be on their way to Vietnam—prepared or not. Four other guys from Cincinnati were in my platoon. I'd never met them before AIT, but we became good friends during the three months at Fort McClellan.

Once again, I couldn't wait for this phase of my training to be over—except for the fact of where I'd be probably be going after it was complete.

I'll never forget standing in our final formation at AIT as they called out orders for our next assignment. The five of us from Cincinnati, by some stroke of luck, were told to report to Fort Benning for scout-dog training. As you can imagine, I was really excited to know I wasn't headed to Vietnam. I figured I'd have a job walking a dog inside the perimeter of an Army camp, maybe in the US.

Remember my friend Tim and my ability to predict the future? Well, I soon found out that what I thought my job would be was just as accurate of a guess!

Putting Earrings on a Pig

I'm sure you've heard the phrase "putting earrings on a pig." You can act like you've changed or have a new idea, but it's usually little more than dressing something up to look or sound different. Underneath, it's still the same old thing.

AIT was nothing more than another version of basic training. The pig might've been fancier, but it was still a pig. It was just wearing earrings.

When life isn't working as well as you'd like, it's easy to look for the next best thing—the fancier pig. You might wait to win the lottery, hope to catch a big break, or rely on an "expert" to give you the answers.

If you're looking for an expert, you'll have no problem finding one. So many "experts" claim to have the answers. If you don't believe me, just watch the morning news shows! Every morning, you can tune in for expert advice on relationships, the stock market, or how to deep-fry a turkey. Some experts are the real deal, but many are simply self-proclaimed authorities.

These experts use the same tactics I experienced in basic training and AIT—wearing you down or creating fear, and then telling you, "We have the answer to your dilemma." When the stock market was booming, the experts knew the stocks to pick: "Trust us! After all, we're the experts." When the market crashed, the experts said they were caught by surprise just like everyone else. Are they really the experts, or are they just like everyone else?

After my Army service, I became a pipefitter. I knew I'd never get rich working as a pipefitter, so I earned my real-estate license in the 1980s. My plan was to make extra money by selling homes and buying rental property.

The market was terrible, and mortgage rates were at 16 percent. My brother-in-law and I bought houses. We fixed up some and flipped them; others we rented.

I grew tired of how difficult it was to sell my listings, and I hated the aggravation of irresponsible renters. So I got out of the business. I felt as if I wasn't prepared to deal with the responsibilities that went with being successful in real estate.

It's funny how easy it is to forget what you know when things look good again! I'm no real-estate expert, but I forgot that. So I thought I'd get back in the game in the mid-2000s, when the market was hot. During the financial boom years, I bought rental property with no money down.

I knew the bubble had to burst eventually. But, like most people, I thought I could ride it out and beat the odds. Of course, the market tanked. Now everyone wants to act like they didn't know the boom years were too good to be true. Most want to act as if the experts fooled them.

The experts didn't fool me. *I* fooled me. You see, I wanted to forget what I learned twenty years earlier by thinking I was a little smarter now. Was I any more prepared? No! New earrings, same pig. (By the way, if you're looking for rental property, I have some for sale at a good price. Trust me. I'm an expert!)

When times are bad, things are going to get better. But as they get better, don't forget and fall prey to the old traps that are dressed up to look different. If it's too good to be true, it's too good to be true. Watch out for the experts waiting to show you a shortcut. True success always involves more hard work than it does shortcuts.

Just like my experience in AIT, we all face situations where we're under pressure and think we need to perform. You may feel like you're being tested by the experts and that you're jumping through hoops.

When I completed AIT, they said I was prepared. But I sure didn't feel as if I was ready. In the end, I didn't respect or trust the experts I was training under.

If you want to be an expert, I suggest you begin with your own life. When you take the time to become a professional at living, you'll become the expert that others are seeking. Actually doing what you want to do with your life is the best preparation you can have for being successful and influencing others.

Given the opportunity to give advice or lead by example, I always choose the latter.

Advice is cheap. Being an example is priceless.

Going to the Dogs

After a thirty-day leave and a much-needed rest, my four new friends and I left Cincinnati and headed to Fort Benning, Georgia. What a difference Scout Dog School was from basic training and AIT! When we arrived, we were treated like human beings.

Life seemed good for scout-dog handlers compared with what was going on around us. Our barracks were located in the same complex with Officer Candidate School (OCS) and Airborne School. OCS and Airborne trainees were ordered to run everywhere, and OCS trainees had to salute everyone they came in contact with. We just had to train our dogs and be trained ourselves. We were off every evening at five o'clock and could do what we liked on the weekends. It was such a drastic change from my first six months in the Army, I almost was afraid that it was a set-up.

Our scout-dog trainers had a completely different approach. They taught us how to do our job—rather than intimidating us and proving they had the power.

It didn't take long for our trainers to sit down with us and describe exactly what a scout-dog team does in the field. The key word in the last sentence is "field."

Let me bring you up-to-date on the job of a scout-dog handler. Remember how I thought I was going to guard a military complex with my dog? Well, it wasn't going to be exactly what I envisioned. We were learning to walk point—first man on patrol—in Vietnam. Along with our dogs, we would learn how to detect the enemy and give an early alert to dangerous situations.

In ninety days, I would be in Vietnam walking point with my dog.

We had about thirty guys in my unit at Scout Dog School and another twenty Marines training with us. One of the duties I pulled that first week was feed detail. Another guy and I had to feed all fifty dogs, which were chained to stakes in the ground. Each dog was in its own small area separated by three-foot-high concrete walls, with a cage door in front of each dog's space, fencing in the rear, and nothing on top. The dogs were waiting for their handlers to be selected and for their training to begin.

The weather was cold, and I wore leather gloves as I gave each dog his bowl of food. All we had to do was to mix the food in a bowl and slide it into the area where the dog was chained. I was about halfway through my first feeding when, as I slid the bowl in close to a black-haired dog, he grabbed my hand. I didn't know what to do. He was pulling me into his area, and I couldn't pull back for fear I'd rip open my hand as his teeth penetrated my glove.

I was really afraid. This wasn't a good situation.

But as quickly as he bit my hand, he let go, and I hastily retreated from his area. I was lucky that I wore leather gloves with liner inserts; I only received puncture wounds.

Chico was the dog who bit me, and that wasn't the last I'd see of him. We had to interact frequently during the next few months. Chico was quite a handful for his handler—no pun intended. Chico looked for every opportunity to ambush anyone who got in his space, so I was very aware and stayed clear of him.

Over the next three months, our dogs learned to alert for people by scent while each handler learned the alert signals given by his dog. We trained the dogs with a pretty simple procedure. When I was ready to scout with my dog, I took off his choke collar and replaced it with a scouting harness, just like the harnesses you buy for pet dogs.

We practiced in different terrains at the base so the dog-and-handler teams could learn in a variety of settings. Five or six of us hid as decoys along the route set out that day. We hid in the grass or brush, waiting for the team to arrive. In the beginning, the dogs didn't know what they were hunting and usually wouldn't give an alert. So when a dog came close to a decoy, the soldier jumped up and startled the dog. Immediately, the soldier would run, and the scout-dog team would chase for a short distance. The decoy then yelled, "Break!" to signal the end of the chase. The decoy turned left and dropped to the ground, while the handler went to the right, praised his dog, and resumed scouting.

It didn't take long for the dogs to become very excited when we put the scouting harnesses on them.

Our dogs were also trained to alert on tripwires—thin wire stretched across a path and tied to explosives. A dog's sight is very good, and they can see the wire vibrate, which happened often because of the wind.

While the dogs used sight and hearing, scent was the key to early detection and warning of imminent danger. Soon our dogs used their keen noses to hunt for decoys, and they picked up the scent of decoys hiding ahead. They also picked up the scent left behind from the person who set a dummy trap with wire and explosives.

While the dogs learned their jobs, the handlers learned to interpret what was going on with their dogs.

My dog's name was Rommel, and his alert was like he was sniffing a delicious steak—except it was a human decoy ahead. My job was to read Rommel's alert at the exact time he gave it. I also had to determine the direction and speed of the wind. Timing is everything when it comes to reading an alert. My dog could alert when a gust of wind changed, and, if I didn't pay attention, my assessment would say the alert was coming from the wrong direction.

The final factor to consider was the strength of the alert and the density of the terrain. In other words, if Rommel had a strong alert in open terrain with a good wind, the human decoy may be 2000 meters ahead. The same type of alert in dense terrain would mean the person was 50 meters in front of us.

The longer I worked with Rommel, the more I learned about his behavior and how to read his signals. He had a pleasant temperament, which made my job much easier than having a more hostile dog like Chico. Some of the dogs we trained with were too aggressive and were sent to Sentry Dog School—the school I originally thought I was signed up for, which trained soldiers for guard duty inside a camp.

For three months, I spent half my time as a decoy for other dogs, like Chico, to hunt. The rest of my time was spent training my dog, Rommel.

At the end of scout-dog training, we were required to run an obstacle course to assess our team's performance. Rommel was a great scout dog. But on the day of the final assessment test, he had a bug and wasn't feeling well. He walked though a couple of tripwires and missed a decoy. While I thought I was prepared, the end result—like many events in my life—was failure.

My training was over, and the day I dreaded was here—I graduated from Scout Dog School. I received orders to report to Oakland, California, in thirty days, when I would ship out to the Republic of Vietnam.

We would spend a week at a temporary duty station after arriving in Vietnam. Our dogs would be waiting for us there. If Rommel stayed behind because of his performance on the final test, a new dog would be assigned to me. I wasn't sure if Rommel would go to Vietnam with me, but I really hoped he would. Rommel and I were a good team.

In thirty days, my greatest fear would come true.

I'd be in Vietnam.

Walking to the Edge

Most big events have a jumping-off point or some kind of "last hurrah." Scout Dog School was my last hurrah before going to Vietnam. We all face jumping-off points in life. And we often want the last hurrah to last a little longer so we don't have to venture into the unknown.

Believe me, I know what I'm talking about!

Since the fall of 1994, I've been the CEO and executive director of Life Success Seminars Inc., a nonprofit personal-development organization founded in 1985 and headquartered in Cincinnati. For thirteen years, Jim Quinn was the lead facilitator for Life Success. Jim was the face of Life Success's first-level seminar, which is called Basic. In fact, Jim was seen by many as the organization itself. After so many years as the lead facilitator, Jim was the only person most people could imagine in that role.

Four years after taking a position at Life Success, I faced a jumping-off point. And I didn't have time for a last hurrah before walking to the edge.

In July 1998, Jim unexpectedly passed away, and I made a decision that's still controversial for some of the nonprofit's founders. I decided I was the most qualified to facilitate our Basic seminar, and I stepped into the position while still running the day-to-day of the organization.

I didn't know how the graduate base would react to Jim's death. I didn't know if they'd still support our seminars and refer people to Life Success.

The grads did continue to support the organization and kept sending their friends, family, and coworkers to our Basic seminar. But the decision came with its challenges, including people who opposed my holding multiple positions as both the organization's leader and lead facilitator. Some people said that I had too much power—I'm still not sure exactly what that means! What exactly did I have power over?

In the end, I was willing to walk up to the edge and face the unknown. I've now facilitated the Basic seminar for Life Success longer than Jim did. When I made my decision, I had no way of knowing how it would work out. But I was prepared to make the decision and make the decision right.

That's what leadership is all about.

All of us are faced with these jumping-off points. And keep in mind that walking to the edge never ends. Should I start a business? Get married? Have a family? These are just a few examples of decisions we all face—decisions we make when we can't possibly know the outcomes.

Walking point—taking the lead—isn't just something that's done in war. It's what you do in life.

Are you willing to take the lead, walk to the edge, and move forward—even if you're not sure you're prepared?

Abandon the safety of your mind and experience the greatness of life.

California Dreaming

I was ordered to report to Oakland, California, and then on to Vietnam. That thirty-day leave between scout-dog training and showing up in California was overwhelming, to say the least. I was so happy to be home for a month. But I didn't really enjoy my time off because I couldn't escape the thought that I was going to Vietnam.

I couldn't help but think that I should've joined the Marines with Tim on the buddy plan—I'd be in Twentynine Palms, California, and not heading for Vietnam!

I considered spending a few extra days at home and showing up late in Oakland. After all, what would the Army do? Send me to Vietnam? I still wasn't prepared to accept my fate, but I decided that I'd just be prolonging my agony. I should move forward.

So my four Cincinnati buddies and I arrived in California a day early, decided to see the sights in Oakland, and reported to our duty station on time. As I think back, I don't remember seeing any sights but I'm sure we saw something—probably a bar or two. I was preoccupied with the idea that in twenty-four hours I would be in Vietnam. Just as I missed experiencing my thirty-day leave, I missed my last day stateside.

The next morning, May 13, 1969, we reported for processing. I remember standing on a huge blacktop area at Travis Air Force Base with what seemed to be thousands of other soldiers. Arriving on time was a good thing. As we stood in formation and our names were called, anyone who wasn't present was considered a deserter. As I said, I'd thought about taking a few extra days of leave. I would've never considered being late that day as an act of desertion, but that gives you a feel for the tone of the times.

I still have my boarding pass, so I know the date I left for Vietnam. But, as I said earlier, I can no longer recollect portions of my story. We flew to Vietnam on a commercial airliner contracted to fly Army troops to Vietnam. I only remember two things about the flight, which were the places we landed.

We landed in the Philippines and on Wake Island. I remember Wake Island because I sat by a window, and, as the plane descended, it looked like we were going to land in the ocean. When we touched down, the runway was so narrow that the wing of the airplane hung over the water. At first, I thought we were in trouble. This was my first trip over the ocean, and I can't swim.

I remember thinking, *This is just my luck. I'm about to die in a plane wreck on my way to getting killed in Vietnam!*

I was so preoccupied with the idea that I really was headed for Vietnam—prepared or not—that I missed most of the flight. But while I recall little about my in-flight time, the landing in Vietnam that I described at the beginning of the book is etched in my soul.

Missing the Journey

Life is funny sometimes: If you don't pay attention, you can miss the journey. I was so worried about what would happen once I arrived in Vietnam, I missed the trip. I doubt I missed much on the way to Vietnam. But in everyday life, if you're distracted, the odds of missing the most important things are much greater.

In the seminars I teach, I work with many people who are wildly successful but aren't very happy. They achieved their goals, but they missed all the fun along the way.

I meet people who made financial wealth their goal but destroyed their health because they were so stressed about earning money. I see good people spend countless hours at work because they're obsessed with being the family provider; they end up divorced because they didn't have time for their spouses and children. I meet parents who say they're teaching responsibility to their children, but they really want to control their lives; eventually, they lose their love and respect. I work with people who don't have time for their friends, and they become disengaged from their circle of influence.

In other words, I work with people who are so busy getting prepared that they're never present in their lives.

It's easy to think everything will take care of itself. I thought good enough was good enough, but my wife, Nancy, wanted more from life and from me. She decided she was going to find a better way to a better life. In May 1987, with her dad's encouragement, Nancy participated in the Basic seminar from Life Success, a group I didn't know much about yet.

After she went to the personal-development seminar, I could see a big change in her. I knew that meant things were going to change for me. But I wasn't sure what I needed to change. I wanted to keep our marriage just the way it was. I didn't want to work any harder on the relationship.

I was coasting in our marriage. I was missing the journey.

I decided to participate in the seminar in order to find a solution, but it's not what you might think. I wanted to learn what Nancy had learned so I could beat her at it! While I attended for selfish reasons, I left the Basic seminar with many tools to improve my marriage and every area of my life.

When I participated in Basic in June 1987, not only did I look at my marriage but I also made a slight shift that brought my Vietnam experiences to the forefront. I'd spent seventeen years keeping silent on what I felt about the war. I would talk occasionally about Vietnam but, for the most part, I figured that it was over and done.

Up to this point, I wasn't prepared to take a deeper look and discuss my feelings about most things, including Vietnam. I started that process during the seminar weekend.

The Basic seminar changed my life. I started living differently in small ways that ended up transforming my entire life. I made a one-degree shift that weekend, and I've kept making one-degree shifts. All together, those small shifts add up to big change. Twenty-five years later, my life is pretty amazing!

When I went to the seminar, I was a union pipefitter. I believed that the life I was living was the best it could be. I believed that I wasn't smart enough to do other things. I didn't like what I was doing, but I felt stuck. I was going to hold out for another twenty years and then retire.

What a great life plan!

Basic changed my plan because I saw the possibility of hope that weekend. I was in a room with successful people who were living life differently than I did. As I experienced the four-day seminar, I realized that I was as competent as anyone in that room. Some people were smarter and more successful than I was, but I was capable of achieving just like they were.

I didn't have to miss the journey.

Life certainly has moments where I have to do more than I expected, and I become distracted. There's always extra work that I didn't sign up for but needs to be done. I just don't have to get lost in the activity.

I didn't join the Army—I was drafted. I didn't choose my circumstances, but I could decide how I wanted to handle myself. We can be present, even when we're involved in things that are out of our control. We don't have to miss the journey.

Most people headed to California in the 1960s for new opportunities, but I went there for a different reason—and it didn't look like an opportunity. You'll find that happens often in life; everyone shows up, but not for the same reasons. Oddly enough, most people I meet miss being present and miss opportunities because of self-judgment.

The enemy is the voice that lives in their head.

What I've learned over the past twenty-five years is how to stay present even when life is busy. I don't have to miss the journey!

There's a famous saying: "When you don't know where you're going, every road leads there." When you're not prepared, it's easy to get lost and miss what's happening.

Be prepared to get lost in the journey of life.

The Reunion

After the long flight to Vietnam and the long wait near Bien Hoa Air Base, I wanted to move on and get situated. My ride finally arrived to take me to the holding kennels where I'd meet up with my dog. This was the main area where all the scout dogs arrived in Vietnam.

I was happy to move forward and leave the area where I kept dwelling on the fear that I might not catch a flight back home.

We were told to put away our gear and report in formation in one hour. I could hear the dogs barking in the kennels. In an odd way, they made me more relaxed. It seemed like I was home.

An hour later, we assembled and the staff sergeant gave us our instructions. We would remain in this camp for one week, working with our dogs on basic obedience and getting them used to the heat. Our respective units would then pick us up. I was given orders for the Forty-sixth Scout Dog Platoon, Twenty-fifth Infantry Division, located near the city of Tay Ninh.

We were told to locate our dogs in the kennel and take them for a walk. If your dog wasn't in the kennel, you'd be assigned a new dog. I searched for Rommel, but he wasn't there. As I suspected, he'd been held back at Fort Benning because he hadn't done well on the final test. I knew he might not be shipped to Vietnam, but I was disappointed.

I walked back to the formation. A few of us were waiting to be assigned dogs. The staff sergeant told us, "I will call out your name, followed by the dog you are assigned."

You've probably figured out what happened next. When my name was called, guess which dog I was assigned?

"Monahan! Chico!"

Remember my old friend Chico? He was the dog who bit me on my first day of feed detail at Fort Benning.

I couldn't believe it. This was just my luck! Chico scared me, and I didn't feel prepared to deal with the hassle of convincing him that we needed to work together. I explained to the sergeant how Chico and I had met. I asked if I could swap Chico for a different dog. After all, I could work with any of the extra dogs in the kennels.

The sergeant told me to get over it. Chico was going to be my dog.

My whole life seems to defy the odds, both good and bad. What are the odds that out of fifty dogs, one would bite me and then later be assigned to me?

If I'd ignored the odds, I could've been with my friend, Tim, in Twentynine Palms, California. Instead, I was in Vietnam with Chico, a dog who hated me.

And that's who I was going to be on the buddy system with for the next year!

We Choose

We don't choose our circumstances in life, but we do choose how we react to those circumstances.

I thought I couldn't catch a break when I found out that Chico was my dog. It was bad enough that I was in Vietnam, walking point for a year. And then I'm assigned a dog that I don't trust!

My attitude wasn't the best. As always, I was letting circumstances dictate my response.

In the first and second grade, Sister Mary Ferdinand was my teacher. Sister Mary Ferdinand was young and took care of me, as if she understood my struggles. I had a hard time in school, but I pushed through the first two years.

Grade three was different.

When I was in the third grade, Sister Mary Lucille was my teacher. I remember Sister Mary Lucille as a short woman in her fifties. That might not accurate, but that's how I remember her.

I didn't do anything differently in the third grade, but I was always in trouble because I was failing. I remember being embarrassed in the first and second grades, but this wasn't the same. Somehow, I'd felt special in grades one and two. But in grade three, I felt different—and not in a good way.

I don't remember anyone helping me at home with my studies. But I do remember getting Fs. I wasn't prepared. Sister Mary Lucille's comments on my report cards included, "Mike does not apply himself" and "Mike is a daydreamer." I quickly decided that these weren't good things.

I failed the third grade, and my opinion of myself changed forever. In September, when all my friends started the fourth grade, I became "stupid."

I reacted to my image of being stupid by not showing up in life, by not taking responsibility. I thought I wasn't prepared, and I was sure that other people would think I was stupid. Until I participated in Life Success's Basic seminar, I always let other people make the decisions. And then I would second-guess their decisions so I could look smart.

In the last twenty-five years, I've worked hard to change this pattern. While my feeling of being stupid has never gone away, I know now that it doesn't dictate my actions. Just because I feel like I'm not completely prepared and that I may fail doesn't mean that I can't go out and do it anyway.

I still battle that image. But I don't have to be a victim of circumstances. I don't have to be a victim of failing the third grade.

As a friend once told me, I should ask everyone whose lives I've touched through my work to send a thank-you note to Sister Mary Lucille. If I hadn't failed the third grade, I'd be doing something entirely different with my life.

I am a victor of failing the third grade.

What circumstances are you holding on to as if they don't have a positive purpose? Life has a bite to it, but the sting eventually goes away. Some people cling to the pain of the bite long after the sting fades.

Life is a choice. Do you see life as a game of chance and circumstances, or do you see life as filled with purpose?

Love Bites

I headed for the kennels and my first official reunion with Chico. As I stood in front of Chico's cage, he seemed pleasant. He wagged his tail and acted very excited to see me. I figured he was ready to make friends. After all, Chico and the other dogs hadn't had contact with anyone in the last thirty days, except for being fed.

Chico seemed to be a different dog than the one I remembered from Fort Benning.

I was rather nervous as I thought about going into his area, but I knew I had to do it sooner or later. I entered Chico's cage and petted him. Things went great! Chico was excited and happy to have someone pay attention to him. As I played with him, I thought that maybe I'd been a little harsh. Our working together would be fine.

I played with Chico for about thirty minutes. I figured that the longer I played with him, the more he would trust me. I decided to take a break and return in a little while to start basic obedience with him.

As I turned to leave the kennel, Chico quickly sunk his teeth into my rear end and then let go, just as quickly. I exited his kennel in disbelief and was filled with dread. While Chico wasn't biting my hand this time, he was picking new areas to bite. That didn't bring me much comfort as to the status of our relationship!

I knew I'd have to take him out of his kennel and begin to work with him, giving commands and correcting his behavior. It was crystal clear that the next phase of our bonding process wasn't going to be received very well by my friend Chico. I thought about going back to the sergeant and asking again if he'd let me trade Chico for another dog. But I knew what he'd say, so I didn't bother asking.

I decided to wait a while to let Chico calm down before working with him. Once again, I started thinking about what I faced over the next year of my life. It was hard not to feel depressed. After all, I was going to walk point for a year and the odds that I'd make it back home weren't that good. If that wasn't bad enough, I now had a new dog—and we didn't like each other.

And my life depended on how good Chico was at doing his job.

I remember thinking that I needed to change my attitude if I had any chance of going home. The Army had done everything it was going to do to prepare me for the next year.

Was I prepared?

I was afraid that I wasn't. Nine months of training sounds like a lot, but I didn't feel as if I was much different than I'd been my whole life. I had a hard time thinking that I might have to kill someone. I just couldn't imagine how I'd feel afterward.

Everything seemed out of my control. And at age twenty, I didn't feel as if I had the skill sets to get my life back on track. That's when I decided that I was going to be the best scout-dog handler I could be. The rest was up to God.

God was in charge because I didn't feel prepared!

Am I Prepared?

Was I prepared for what was about to happen?

I just finished nine months of training, and I faced three big questions in my mind:

1. Am I ready to die at twenty years old?
2. Am I ready to go home missing my legs or some other body parts?
3. Am I ready to kill someone?

After some soul-searching, I concluded that the answer to these three questions was, "I don't know." The only way I would know is when the year was over and I was home.

In life, we learn to prepare for the future. But we often think that preparation will guarantee the outcome we want. While we stand a better chance of achieving the desired outcome if we prepare, we certainly don't have a guarantee.

Have you ever heard the saying, "Life isn't fair"? Successful people prepare to be in a position to make the most out of an uneven playing field. Successful people take advantage of the opportunities that life presents.

Once you realize that no guarantees come with preparation, you may find that you're willing to take more chances, to risk quicker and more often. Successful people are risk takers. When times are bad and everyone else is playing it safe, waiting on things to turn around, risk takers take advantage of opportunities.

Do you want to know the answer to the question, "How will I know when I'm prepared?" When you're finished! When would I know that I was prepared for Vietnam? I would know that I was prepared if I came home, safe or injured. I'd know when I had to kill someone or not. Before all of that happened, I had no way of knowing.

Am I prepared for this book to be a best seller? I'm prepared to do my part to make that happen. But I can't control the outcome.

If you're always prepared, you're missing the adventure.

Am I Safe?

In the beginning of this book, I shared three questions that I asked myself while I was in Vietnam. And I still ask myself these three questions each day:

1. Am I prepared?
2. Am I safe?
3. Am I alone?

I found that "Am I prepared?" would be a work-in-progress. And I was pretty clear that I would struggle with the question, "Am I safe?" while I was in Vietnam. But my challenges with this question didn't end when I came home.

I believe that we all struggle with the question, "Am I safe?" as we face daily life.

You probably hesitate in many areas of your life because you don't feel safe. In the areas you've put on hold, ask yourself this question: "What is the worst thing that could happen if I do this?"

If "die" is one of your answers, you have a great reason for not moving forward! But the other reasons you come up with may not be as solid.

If you do the right thing each day, you'll often ask yourself the safety question. When you do what you love, you'll stand out and be noticed in life. But you'll often feel as if you're in over your head, and that can feel unsafe.

Fear is a feeling. Think about this: Most people aren't living the life they want based on the fact that fear—a feeling—keeps them from taking a risk.

Read this sentence as many times as you need to in order to believe what I'm saying: Feelings don't make you do anything!

Action is a separate choice, regardless of the feelings that you have.

You can be angry and feel as if your boss does not appreciate you. You can sit down and have a civil conversation about it, or you can lash out. It's a choice of action.

We usually don't connect poor communication with feeling unsafe. But almost all communication breakdowns are because you don't understand, you don't trust, and you defend your position. Why? You don't feel safe.

It doesn't matter what position you're currently in. No matter what, you're subconsciously asking the question, "Am I safe?" If you're in the lead, you're wondering if you're making the right decisions. Will people support you so you accomplish what you want to achieve? If you're following, you wonder, "Is it safe to trust the leader? Does he know what he's doing? If he makes the wrong decision, could I lose my job?"

It doesn't matter what area of your life we're talking about. The question remains the same. Should I get married? Will I have enough money to retire? Who will take care of me if I become really sick?

Am I safe?

This question runs much deeper than most people realize. This fear of safety causes a lot of stress and emotional pain.

There's a big difference between feeling unsafe and being in danger. I stay away from what's dangerous and approach what feels unsafe on a daily basis.

Living a great life means you'll feel like you're on the edge!

Do you want to live the life of your dreams or a life of safety? You can't have both!

Let's Get Swinging

Once I decided that I couldn't change my circumstances, all I could do was be the best I could be each day. But I knew that I didn't feel very safe. I wasn't in immediate danger, but my situation wasn't very comforting.

I just had my first interaction with my new dog, and it didn't go well. I'd be using valuable time trying to convince Chico that he wasn't in charge, instead of learning how he scouted. I'd probably be out walking point in a week or two—for the first time—with a dog I didn't know very well.

No wonder I didn't feel safe.

But I knew it was time to quit stalling and pick up my equipment. A six-foot leash and a choke collar were all I needed. Once again, Chico looked excited as I opened the door to his holding cage. His tail wagged a hundred miles an hour as I entered his cage. You would've thought we were best friends by his behavior—if you forgot that he'd just bitten me in the ass an hour earlier.

I slipped the choke collar over his head and down around his neck, snapping on the leash. We were off to train.

Basic obedience was the first course of action. I walked Chico in the heel position, which meant his shoulder should stay next to my right leg. This was a simple command, and Chico was already trained. He didn't need any correction.

The next challenge was when I stopped, because Chico should sit immediately. If Chico decided not to sit, my job was to repeat the command, "Sit," and jerk his leash, which would tighten his choke collar. Seems simple enough, doesn't it?

I just knew it wasn't going to work that way.

After walking for about ten minutes, I stopped. As I suspected, Chico remained standing. I knew that my next move would be the beginning of a test of wills. In the end, I'd have to win the test.

I jerked his leash and gave the command, "Sit!" As his choke collar tightened, Chico reacted. Chico wanted no part of me telling him what to do, much less me jerking his collar. He lunged forward in an attempt to bite my wrist. I needed to take immediate defensive action.

In my training at Scout Dog School, we were taught how to handle a dog trying to attack. When a dog lunges at the handler, the defensive maneuver is to quickly spin the dog around by his leash, keeping all four of his feet off the ground. Eventually, the dog blacks out and you set him on the ground. The idea is to eliminate the dog's ability to lunge and bite, and the dog is confused when he wakes up after blacking out.

I immediately began swinging Chico in circles to keep his legs off the ground. This maneuver isn't easy, and it takes awhile for the dog to black out. Once Chico was out, I set him down. He immediately came to, and I resumed walking and giving him commands all afternoon.

While everyone else was working with their dogs on simple commands, Chico was lunging. All I did was airplane spins with my dog.

After two days, Chico finally gave in and started to follow my commands. Don't get me wrong: Chico didn't give up his attitude. He would still resist my commands and often growled at me, but we had an agreement that he couldn't bite me. Chico was difficult, but we had to find a way to work together or everyone involved in our patrols would be unsafe.

We finished our time in this camp with basic obedience and training on the obstacle course. Later in the week, a couple of guys showed up in a truck to take Chico and me to the Forty-sixth Scout Dog Platoon.

I'd finally get to see my home for the next year!

Working With Difficult People

"The squeaky wheel gets the grease." This saying usually is used in a negative context: People who underperform or complain all the time are the ones who get what they want.

My two daughters used to be restaurant servers. Julie and Coleen worked at different restaurants, but they'd both have trouble with the same thing—other servers who wouldn't help out and do their share. They both complained that some of their coworkers would never polish and roll the silverware that was needed for that evening. Julie and Coleen both talked about how if they were really busy, the slackers wouldn't help.

But these two behaviors were only the tee up to what drove my girls absolutely crazy. Every now and then, business would be slow on a Friday night and the manager would send home a few servers. The manager always let the underperformers go home. Julie and Coleen would rant for hours: "I can't believe he let her off on a Friday! I haven't had a Friday off in ages!"

Once in awhile, after they finished complaining, I'd ask: "If you owned the restaurant and you had customers you cared about, would you keep your best servers or the difficult servers?" They'd usually roll their eyes and say, "I know, Dad! But it's just not fair!"

Chico and I didn't like each other, but I didn't have the luxury of saying, "It's not fair, so I'm not going to do my best." My life depended on our relationship working.

The reality is that we often are in difficult situations with difficult people. When you don't trust someone, it's hard to feel safe. But if we don't take personal responsibility, we become just like those we complain about. Their actions don't control your behavior. Are you going to do what's right? That's what really matters.

Everybody is looking for the best partner, but who's going to be the first to be the best partner? Everyone is looking to be on the best team, but are you showing up as the best player you can be? Everybody wants to be forgiven, but are you going to forgive?

Remember that you're destined to fail if you're looking for life to be fair or equal.

If there was a list of the world's most difficult people, we might be surprised to see our own names near the top! For all the reasons you think someone else is difficult, they might be seeing *you* as the difficult person. Maybe they feel unsafe with you.

So what do you do with difficult people? Just like I had to find a way to be with Chico, you might have to find a way to deal with people you don't like. Can you come to an agreement so you both get to where you're going?

Difficult people usually aren't reasonable, so save your reasonability for a thoughtful person. When a reasonable person argues with an unreasonable person, you always end up with two unreasonable people. Don't join the Difficult People Club—it's already overcrowded!

Feeling safe around others is usually more about you than them.

In the Doghouse

The ride to Tay Ninh and the Forty-sixth Scout Dog Platoon took a couple of hours. For much of the drive, the roads were lined with American tanks because it wasn't safe to travel without protection. I was getting the idea that Vietnam wasn't a place to relax—playing it safe was wise.

The two men who picked up Chico and me seemed like pretty good guys. One of the two was a sergeant and when I called him "Sergeant," he told me to drop the title and call him by his first name. I later found out that rank in Vietnam didn't carry the same weight as it did in the US. Vietnam was more like the Wild West—anything goes.

As soon as we arrived, I took Chico out of his cage and over to the dog kennels. The platoon had a vet tech—an apprentice veterinarian—who did a quick check to make sure Chico was okay.

After I put Chico in his cage, I reported to the first sergeant. After a brief overview of the platoon, he told me to get situated in the barracks. He gave me a set of patches for the Forty-sixth Scout Dog Platoon and told me to go to the tailor and have the patches sewn on my fatigues that day.

I located a room and began to put my gear away. After I talked with a few guys who came and introduced themselves, I felt a bit tired and decided to take a short nap. Well, the short nap turned into a long nap. And the long nap was followed by dinner. After eating, I realized that the tailor shop was closed. I figured this wasn't a big deal—I could take care of it the next day.

The next morning, when we lined up in formation, the first sergeant saw that I didn't have my patches sewn on my fatigues. He went crazy. For me, the patches weren't a big deal. But for him, this was a really big deal. That was the beginning of his "I'm-going-to-be-your-worst-nightmare relationship" with me.

To show how unhappy he was with me, he put me on shit detail. No, it's not a metaphor—it's the real thing. The latrine had four toilet seats mounted on plywood and under each seat was a fifty-five-gallon drum cut down to about twenty-four inches high. Each drum had two inches of fuel oil in the bottom.

I soon learned that each morning someone—me—would take a hook and drag all four drums out from under the latrine openings. Once the drums were far enough away from the latrine, more fuel oil and a small amount of gasoline were added and the drums lit. Eventually, the fire would burn out and that day's shit was taken care of. Just like spraying a skillet, I'd pour a couple of inches of fuel oil in the drums and return them to their proper places under the latrine seats, ready for a whole new day of shit.

The first sergeant was in charge for about six months after I arrived, and I was his "pet." He would show his favoritism for me by putting me on shit detail anytime I was in from the field and back in our platoon. I eventually just skipped formation and went straight to the latrine for shit duty.

I have a bit of an authority-figure problem. I didn't want this guy to think he was getting to me, so I burned the shit without being ordered to. I didn't want him to have the satisfaction of telling me to do it. I knew he would watch me to see if I was aggravated by the detail. Sometimes, just for the hell of it, I would stir the shit while it was burning, treating it like a fine pot of stew. I was hoping *he* would stew!

It's funny how life works. As bad as shit detail was, it was a distraction from the reality of my life. For a short time, I could forget I was afraid that I might die at any moment. Hating the first sergeant and burning shit provided a strange comfort.

Fighting Back

When I was drafted into the Army, the training was designed to break me so I would follow those who had higher rank. While I was in the US, authority was used to control me through fear. It worked. I didn't feel safe, and I was afraid of the consequences for not following orders in basic training and AIT.

After I was in Vietnam, I wasn't very afraid of the consequences. What were they going to do? Send me to Vietnam? I'm already there! What else could they do? Dock my pay forty dollars a month? I could die at any moment, and I should worry about forty dollars? I don't think so!

In Vietnam, life was about trust and respect—not rank and authority. When you look at families or businesses, many operate in much the same way. Some people want to control others with fear and threats, while others want to inspire by leading and being an example.

An "authority figure" to me is anyone trying to tell me what to do. And my job is to fight them. This is a pretty simple formula to live by, except this theory also includes fighting people who are trying to give me good advice. Even if it's good advice, it's still telling me what to do. So I fight them.

I don't know about you but, in my life, it's been rather easy to start off on the wrong foot. In my first marriage, I started with no money, a lack of skill sets, and a bunch of kids in diapers. When I was a pipefitter, I always bucked the system. As a result, I was often laid off or in trouble.

While I was in the pipefitters union, I held several leadership positions and served on many committees. Every time I ran for a union position, I was elected. I was well liked. I liked my beer, and I appealed to the rebellious members of the union. But after participating in a Life Success seminar in 1989, I quit drinking. And I was ready to quit fighting.

I was serious about wanting to move forward as a leader in the union, and I was given a big job—as general foreman on a project—that would really help my political career.

The job ended up being one of those circumstances that I wished I didn't have to face. After a few months, the project superintendent told me that I needed to sign off on some instruments as installed—but the instruments hadn't been installed yet. He said it was standard operating procedure, but it didn't feel right to me. I wouldn't sign off.

My first instinct was to fight the issue, but the superintendent had already done several things behind my back. I didn't trust him. A few days later, I quit because I didn't think it was healthy for me to work with this guy. This job jeopardized the safety of what I wanted to do differently in my life.

When I went back to the union hall, the business agent who gave me the job told me I was shooting myself in the foot by quitting. He said this was the biggest political mistake that I'd ever make. My dilemma was that I could fight or walk—and neither felt very good.

The business agent was right. Later that year, when I ran for union business agent, I lost to the guy who replaced me as general foreman on the job I had quit. And if that wasn't bad enough, I came in dead last in a field of four candidates.

I was so angry that I couldn't see straight. I was tired of working as a pipefitter, and the election was my big chance to be a leader and get out of the day-to-day labor. Just like being in Vietnam, I felt as if I couldn't survive the loss of the election.

How was I going to change my attitude? And what was I going to do next with my life?

I didn't choose a dishonest superintendent, just like I didn't choose Chico or the first sergeant. But I did get to choose how I was going to deal with the circumstances that were dealt to me.

For six months, I struggled with being very angry. I wanted to move on, but I was acting like a victim of circumstances. The truth is, I was the one who quit the job—and it was for the right reasons. But I didn't like the consequences of my decision. I didn't like how the circumstances played out.

Like shit detail, I had to find a way to deal with the situation differently. In the end, I was proud that I chose to quit instead of just fighting to prove the superintendent wrong. Quitting was the right thing for me to do.

How much time do you spend fighting in your marriage, with your children, or at work? How many of those battles are about your ego being threatened and you feeling unsafe? If you're not in danger and it's just about being right, why bother?

Fighting is more about fear than what you're fighting for.

Time to Go Into the Field

Within a couple of days, it was time to leave my platoon and go into the field. Scout-dog teams worked on a rotating basis. We'd be in the field, on patrol, for five days and then back in base camp with our platoon for at least two days of rest. The rest was for our dogs, not for the soldiers. Remember, I burned shit when I was in camp!

The first time I went into the field, I went with another dog team and I just watched. The second time I went on patrol, I took my dog and an experienced scout-dog handler observed me. After that patrol, Chico and I would be entirely on our own.

For my first patrol, I would be observing a scout-dog handler who was nicknamed "Squanto." Squanto was quite a character—and he was the best horseshoe player I've ever seen in my life. He threw fifteen straight ringers in camp one night. Anyway, Squanto spent some time with me before going into the field for the first time. He told me everything I needed to pack for five days, and this would be the lightest I'd ever pack for a patrol. For all future patrols, I'd have to carry food and water for Chico, in addition to carrying my own gear.

In the morning, a truck took us to the airfield to catch a chopper that would take us to a fire support base and the company we were assigned to for five days. Our platoon was in base camp, the main camp near Tay Ninh. Six fire support bases surrounded base camp. The idea was that base camp could support all six of the fire support bases, and that each fire support base could support the fire support base on either side of it, as well as supporting the base camp.

Soon we were on a chopper, and I was headed to my first fire support base. I was excited and afraid at the same time. But the fire support base we went to wasn't anything to write home about—it was rather small. The chopper landed outside the base and the entire perimeter was defended with barbed wire and claymores (antipersonnel mines). We entered through an opening in the wire that was closed each night.

Once inside the perimeter, I saw that the base had a command bunker for all communications. (Bunkers are reinforced underground shelters.) A series of manned perimeter bunkers defended the base. Squanto and I slept in a bunker that night. And it was clear to me that the fire support base didn't have the same level of safety as base camp.

A first lieutenant came to the bunker and told Squanto that we should be at a briefing at 0700 hours (7 a.m.). According to Squanto, sometimes the company commander wanted the scout-dog team to attend the morning briefings; other times, we weren't invited. It all depended on the company.

The next morning, Squanto and I went to the briefing and were told that we would be picked up by an eagle flight. An eagle flight usually featured eight helicopters, including four choppers that flew side-by-side, one or two Cobra helicopters for fire support, and an LOH (a two-seat light-observation helicopter) that flew low to draw fire. We were going to patrol an area suspected of being a North Vietnamese Army (NVA) or Viet Cong (VC) encampment. (The VC were communist guerillas that fought with the support of the NVA.)

Squanto, his dog, and I walked with the company a short distance to a clearing to wait for the eagle flight to arrive. We spread out so that when the choppers touched down, we'd be in position to get on one of them. The helicopters arrived, and Squanto instructed me to stick close to him. We ran to one of the choppers, and, to my surprise, we sat in the doorway with our feet hanging out. Three of us sat on our side, plus a door gunner who was a member of the chopper crew. Each helicopter usually held eight guys. We quickly were in the air, headed for our destination.

Eventually, the choppers started descending toward the landing zone (LZ) where we'd begin our patrol. As we approached the LZ, all hell broke loose. The door gunners opened fire, and Squanto's dog barked like crazy because the machine-gun noise hurt his ears. As the choppers touched down, everybody jumped off, hit the ground, and fired their M16s.

What happened next startled me. As quickly as the shooting started, it ended. Squanto got up off the ground as if nothing had happened, and he told me to get up and come with him. As I stood up, I asked him, "What just happened?" Squanto replied, "I forgot to tell you that this is a hot LZ." When Army intelligence believes the enemy is in the area, he said, we go in shooting.

I'd just experienced my first hot LZ.

I'm not sure Squanto was telling me the truth. I think he "forgot" to tell me about the hot LZ just to give me a heart attack on my first day in the field! And he accomplished his goal because it was crystal clear: Did I feel safe? No!

Squanto had a short discussion with the platoon leader about where we were headed, and we were all soon on our way. Squanto walked point with his dog, and I walked next to him. The platoon stayed behind us as we patrolled. As we walked, Squanto watched his dog and talked with me. We walked for several hours, headed for an area believed to be a large bunker complex that housed the NVA or VC.

We reached a wooded area that quickly turned into jungle terrain, with trails leading into the dense vegetation. Trails usually weren't used by US patrols because the paths were often booby-trapped. Two guys were assigned to start chopping a new path just off to the side of the main trail. The terrain was so thick, it took forever to chop our way through the vegetation. The captain finally made the decision to return to the main trail and walk it with a great deal of caution.

Squanto moved with care as we walked the trail and went deeper into the jungle. As we continued, we noticed that the trail was lined on both sides with bunkers. This was obviously a major enemy staging area. Not only was it dangerous to be walking the trail, but we also had the added factor that the enemy might still occupy some bunkers.

It seemed like we walked for miles, and the area was thick with enemy bunkers. After about an hour, we came to a large clearing. This was the center of the bunker complex, and trails went off in four directions. Most of our patrol gathered in the center of the camp, and the captain discussed the situation with his platoon leaders.

The captain called to Squanto, "Dog man, come here!" We walked over to the captain and Squanto addressed him, "Yes, sir!" The captain asked Squanto, "How long have they been gone?" Squanto bent down and picked up a discarded cigarette pack that the enemy had left behind. He pointed to the cigarette pack and explained: "The way the sun is coming through the canopy and from the discoloration of this cigarette pack, I would say they've been gone forty-eight to seventy-two hours." The captain thanked him and immediately got on the radio to report back to the command center.

Squanto and I went to the side of the clearing and sat down to take a break while the captain decided what we'd do next. As we sat there, I told Squanto how impressed I was with his ability to assess the situation beyond working with his dog. I was curious where he'd learned about the effects of the sun on the cigarette pack and determining the time related to the enemy leaving. I also explained that I didn't recall learning anything like that at Scout Dog School at Fort Benning.

Squanto looked at me with a grin and said, "I made it up!"

"What do you mean you made it up?" I replied. "Are you crazy?"

"The way I see it," Squanto said, "the Vietnamese are gone, and it doesn't matter if they've been gone five minutes or five years. The important thing is that they're gone. And right now, that captain thinks I'm the smartest guy he's ever met!"

Squanto was right. The Vietnamese were long gone—and how long didn't matter. He was also right about the captain: He treated Squanto as if he was a genius the rest of the time we worked with the platoon!

Making It Up

Squanto taught me a great lesson that day. At the time, I just thought that what happened was funny. But I later learned to use what he taught me. And my guess is that I learned more from Squanto's actions than he did.

Squanto taught me that it was okay to make it up. I didn't need to take the safety route all the time.

When you're in a leadership position, you'll find that you sometimes have to convince your team about something that *you* aren't even sure about. That's part of being a vision person—make up something and persuade others to make it happen.

That may be an oversimplification, but no matter how much you plan, there's always an element of guesswork.

Back when I was a pipefitter, I started a new job at the same time as another pipefitter named Joe. When we walked in on the first day, the foreman told us it was just about break time, and he led Joe and me to the break area. As we walked, we passed a work area with stacks of clean, chrome pipe. It looked like it would be good work. The foreman asked me if I'd ever worked with that type of pipe. "Yes, I have," was my response. "After break, you and Joe meet me in that area, and we'll go over the blueprints," he said.

When the foreman left, I told Joe that we needed to find somebody who had worked with that kind of pipe and knew what they were doing, because I didn't. Joe couldn't believe what I'd done. I told Joe, "This is simple. We just find someone here who has worked with this pipe before and ask them to explain what we need to know."

And if no one knew how to install the pipe, I figured that we weren't any dumber than anyone else on the job!

One of the other guys, who happened to be a buddy of mine, told us what we needed to know. Joe and I had a nice, clean job for six months.

My job at Life Success is to create a vision for the nonprofit and work with the board of trustees to implement an action plan to move the organization forward. Really smart people are on this board, and they're looking to me to provide leadership.

When I'm running Life Success, I often feel as if I'm driving a train at one hundred miles per hour as I'm laying the track in front of the train!

If you're running a business—or raising a family—you'll have times when you just have to make it up. And you will feel unsafe.

If you're going to be an expert, at some point you'll have to give up your safety and look like the expert—even before you are one. And let's face it: We're all making up things in an attempt to get what we want.

Sometimes you have to move beyond "being reasonable" and risk putting an idea out there. Then you need to put wings to it after you've launched the idea. That's why we call those made-up ideas "dreams." Dreams capture our imaginations.

When you don't feel safe, it's almost impossible to imagine. Ideas, images, dreams. Just make it up!

Imagination is dangerous to a reasonable mind. You have to sacrifice safety to live the dream.

Landings and Take-Offs

Vietnam was a strange war. We really never took any territory—we just patrolled.

Imagine a city with a downtown area and many suburbs. Downtown is your home, your base camp. Each day, you patrol one suburb and then return home. The next day, you patrol another suburb and then go home again. You may go back to the same suburb several times during a six-month period.

That's what we did in Vietnam, day in and day out. Talk about frustrating the troops!

We not only didn't take territory, but we also patrolled in many areas where we were restricted to returning fire—we had to be fired upon first. Free fire zones were where we could shoot at will, but we often weren't in free fire zones.

I remember many times when I was leading a patrol and, out of nowhere, we'd come upon Vietnamese farmers or people cutting wood. We didn't know if they were the enemy or not.

The enemy looked just like our allies. We had to wait to be shot at before we could take action.

Do you think any of us ever felt safe?

Safe or not, we had a mission each day we were in the field. We usually flew on choppers to the areas we were going to patrol. As I said earlier, these helicopter formations were called eagle flights.

Eagle flight pilots didn't like to sit on the ground for long. We were told ahead of time what type of landing we faced both when being dropped off and picked up. For example, we were told quite a few times that when we were picked up, the landing would be a tap-and-go. The choppers would come in quickly, touch down, and almost immediately take off. I often saw guys hanging on to the chopper skids, being pulled in by their buddies.

Landings were always a high stress time for Chico and me because ground fire was common. Remember the hot LZ my first day that I was in the field? Chico, just like Squanto's dog, went crazy during landings. Dogs' ears are incredibly sensitive, and a door gunner's machine gun is unbelievably loud. As soon as a chopper touched down for a pickup, I ran to be the first one on the chopper. My goal was to get Chico situated so he wasn't biting everyone as they jumped onboard.

While I was part of many landings, some stand out in my mind to this day. On one eagle flight, I was told that we were going into a hot LZ and should expect enemy fire. We weren't going to land—the helicopters would hover above the ground for a few seconds. The chopper copilot would give us the signal to jump.

Eight choppers flew in formation. As we came in to the landing area, the door gunners opened fire. Two support Cobra helicopters were firing. The eagle flight came in quickly and stopped just as quickly. The copilot signaled and, without thinking, I jumped from the chopper as we hovered about six feet above the ground.

My feeling at that moment is stuck in my head. I was the first guy to hit the ground. That may not seem like a big deal—unless you're the one guy on the ground. It seemed like an eternity until I heard another guy land near me. Logically, I know that it was probably just a few seconds between when I jumped and the next guy jumped.

But I remember thinking: *I jumped too quickly. The choppers are pulling out, and I'm being left here all alone.*

Have you ever had that feeling as if you're alone and there's no one but you in the entire world? That's what I felt like when I hit the ground. I felt as unsafe as I've ever been in my life!

I made a promise that day that I would never, ever be the first guy on the ground again. As odd as it sounds, I just needed to know that one person was with me.

Now that I look back, I'd like to believe that the chopper pilots wouldn't have left me behind. But when I was there, it sure seemed like a possibility. As I said earlier, the choppers didn't want to be on or near the ground any longer than necessary.

Survival of the fittest was real to me.

Drop Zone

We often think we're prepared for what's about to happen. But when we hit the drop zone, we usually face surprises—just as I did on that eagle flight landing. We subconsciously ask ourselves, "Am I safe?"

While there might not be an apparent danger, I know that I often don't feel safe or prepared for surprises. But I don't let that stop me.

When I became executive director of Life Success Seminars in 1994, the organization wasn't in good financial shape. As a small nonprofit, we had few donors. We borrowed money from some of our donors so I could make the changes needed to move the organization forward.

But the same people who hired me—the board of trustees—were sometimes the most resistant to the very changes I needed to make.

Within a week of starting, I asked the board president to instruct the board members to stop calling about every decision I made. Three months later, I fired three facilitators—one was a staff member and one was a board member's wife.

A lot of people were very unhappy with the cultural changes I made in the organization. Not only was I fighting the current board, but I also faced resistance from past board members and some of the people who started Life Success.

It was an uphill battle the whole way.

By keeping the staff lean, we recovered from the initial deficit and repaid the loans. As the organization grew, so did our cash reserves.

We were on our way to a brighter future.

During the next few years, we increased participation in our personal-development seminars and expanded our programs. In 1999, Life Success held its first capital campaign. We raised $1.5 million and built a conference center that opened in spring 2003. The West Chester Conference Center is home to our business offices and most of our seminars; we also rent the center for corporate meetings.

The combination of what I learned in Vietnam and at Life Success has helped me have the courage to push through many difficult situations.

The work we do at Life Success is life-changing, and the people who participate are passionate about the organization. But passion works both ways. When people disagree with what I do as the leader, the atmosphere can get rather heated.

When I hit the Life Success "drop zone," I never guessed that I'd face so many surprises. In many cases, if I knew what was going to happen, I might not have shown up in the first place!

Do you find that you resist change because it feels like you're walking on a wire without a net? Taking a risk without a net can feel very unsafe!

Raising children, being married, running a business—all have unbelievable challenges. But these challenges forced me to go beyond my self-imposed limits and safety zones. These challenges made me a better father, husband, and leader.

How many times have you thought, *How did I get in the middle of this mess?* Once we commit to anything, we always face surprises. Many of these surprises will evoke fear. But that doesn't mean you have to stop doing what you're doing.

Every decision you make will have an element of chance attached to the outcome. Don't get lost in the feeling of not being safe in the unknown. Of course it's a bit unsafe—it's the unknown!

Thoughts about future surprises are always scarier than the actual surprises.

Rank: I Don't Think So!

Until I arrived in Vietnam, I thought that rank just had its privileges in the Army. Now that I think about it, rank did have its privileges in Vietnam. I turned twenty-one one month after I arrived in Vietnam, but I couldn't buy liquor because I wasn't ranked high enough. I could die, but I couldn't drink!

But rank in Vietnam just didn't pull the same weight as it did back in the US. In Vietnam, pulling rank—or taking unfair advantage from a superior position—didn't work. As a matter of fact, pulling rank usually was unsafe. And it could get you killed.

Scout-dog teams rotated to different companies. One of the companies I worked with called a briefing on my first morning so we could go over where and what we were going to do on patrol that day. A staff sergeant briefed us on the mission.

The first lieutenant, who ranked above the staff sergeant, stepped in and started to tell us—in an arrogant way—what he wanted us to do that day. He was obviously new to Vietnam. The first clue was the fact that the first lieutenant wore clean, bright fatigues. The second clue was the look on the staff sergeant's face.

As the first lieutenant finished telling us what to do, the staff sergeant looked at him and delivered this message in front of all of us: "Sir, we'll be doing what I tell the men to do. You will follow along, and we will tell you when you're ready to lead us. We aren't going to get anyone killed because you're fresh out of officer school and think you know what's going on over here."

And if that wasn't enough, the staff sergeant finished with: "And if you don't like that, sir, you may not make it back today."

The first lieutenant was quiet the rest of the day!

As I said earlier, the Army in Vietnam had an element of the Wild West. If you didn't like what someone was saying or doing to you, retaliation often followed. One of the ways soldiers retaliated was by "fragging." Soldiers would take a hand grenade and toss it into someone's room while they were sleeping. The intention was to kill them.

This wasn't about throwing grenades at the enemy. I'm talking about killing fellow American soldiers, particularly unpopular senior officers. Fragging was way more common than you might think, so minding your own business was a good idea.

I told you how I didn't get along with the first sergeant when I arrived at the Forty-sixth Scout Dog Platoon. When he left, the first sergeant who replaced him was a goof. The soldiers played basketball right outside his window, and the guys would talk about fragging him—just to make him nervous. He was so worried about it that he slept with a baseball bat and a .45 pistol on his nightstand.

One night, I had phone duty. The desk was on the other side of the new first sergeant's bedroom wall. He came out of his room to talk with me. For some reason, we'd always gotten along and he trusted me.

That night, he asked me if I thought that the guys in the platoon really would frag him. It was a dirty trick on my part, but I said that there was no way they would. When he breathed a sigh of relief, I said, "They won't frag you because it might come through the wall. And they like me and don't want me to be hurt."

Setting him up that way was pretty cruel, but I still smile about it. I guess I haven't changed all that much!

The rules are different in war. When soldiers feel as if they don't have anything to lose, they respond to authority in a completely different way.

When a soldier faces death each day, life becomes unsafe. And if you're not safe, rank and authority no longer intimidate easily.

Authority and Control

It's just a guess, but I bet that you're fragging some of the people around you. You aren't killing people, but you're killing your relationships and killing your results in life.

I set up the first sergeant and jerked the rug out from under him. What are you doing to other people? Maybe a work deadline is coming up and you're holding back so a colleague fails. Or do you keep score in your marriage and friendships? Do you ever think, *It's not my turn to give in?* Would you rather be right than happy?

Most people see how the other person in a relationship lobs grenades, but they never see the grenades they throw. Judgmental, critical, arrogant, skeptical, envious. What's in your grenade arsenal?

Right after Nancy and I married, I'd been off work for more than a year. Sometimes, I'd be off of work because of tough times in the construction business. But I had a tendency to run my mouth a little more than needed, and that added to my demise.

On a Friday, I finally got the call I'd been waiting for. On Monday, I was to report to the sewer plant, where a two-year job was beginning. Nancy and I were really excited that I was going back to work.

We went for a ride on Sunday, and we talked about my new job. I told her that because I'd been off work for so long, I was going to keep my mouth shut. I was going to mind my own business, and I wasn't going to say a word if something didn't pertain to me.

In Nancy's infinite wisdom, she turned to me and asked, "What are you going to do on Tuesday?"

I'd been fragging myself.

When my kids were growing up, I often acted like a dictator. According to Julie, my oldest daughter, "There was no '-tator' to it!" She's right. I was over-the-top with rules and regulations. At the time, I believed that I was teaching them how to be responsible people.

But it really was about control.

I eventually realized that I wanted to control my children's behavior to keep distance in our relationships. My real fear was that if they weren't angry with me, they might love me. If they loved me, did I know how to love them back? And would my love be good enough?

My family didn't express love very much when I was growing up. As an alcoholic, my dad wasn't emotionally available. I didn't have a male role model, so it was easy to act as if I was hard. But I really wasn't hard at all. I loved my kids very much—that's why I wanted custody when my first wife and I divorced. I just didn't know how to show love another way. So I became the authority.

I was fragging my relationships with my kids.

I realized that I had to change or I'd never gain the true respect and love that I wanted from my children. I wanted to change how I was showing up as a father and as a husband.

More than twenty years later, I'm proud of the changes I've made that improved my relationships with all of my children and their spouses. I'm a resource to them, and they share some of their greatest challenges with me. Of all the leadership areas that I've improved, the "father" area is the one I'm most proud of changing.

If you need a verbal weapon to get your way, you're probably at war.

It's a Matter of Conditioning

Many things about Vietnam simply amazed me. For example, I was blown away by how the soldiers who'd been in the country for a while seemed to have total disregard for their own safety.

When I first arrived at my platoon, I was assigned a room in a wooden barracks. Sandbags were laid up to about four feet high around the base of the barracks. The roof was made of corrugated metal, and the structure didn't have any windows—just screens.

Our barracks weren't really built for safety.

In the event of rocket attacks, our platoon had a couple of underground bunkers with bunk beds. Rocket attacks happened three or four times a week, in the evening. As soon as I heard the first rocket hit, I ran for the closest bunker. I expected to see the rest of my platoon below ground, too.

The funny thing is that unless a rocket hit really close to our platoon, the only two people in the bunker were the company clerk and me. As a side note, we were rocketed one night at dinnertime, and the clerk was in the shower. I thought I was afraid, but I didn't hold a candle to him! He came out of the showers and rapidly low-crawled—naked—across the gravel parking lot to the bunker.

For about a month, I went to the bunker to sleep when we were under attack. I didn't feel safe. But many of the soldiers just smoked marijuana and slept through the noise. One guy wore the headphones for his big reel-to-reel tape player so he couldn't hear the rockets.

I remember thinking, *I will never be like those idiots! How can they not care?* Well, it was just a matter of time before sleeping on a hard bed in a smelly, damp bunker with little fresh air lost out to idiotic thinking.

I soon became one of the guys lying in bed in the barracks, listening to rockets hitting and deciding if they were far enough away to stay above ground. The rockets didn't follow a pattern, so guessing how far away they were was as accurate as walking on an expressway blindfolded!

I was amazed by my ability to adapt to the conditions on a physical, mental, and emotional level. When I landed in Vietnam, the heat took my breath away and I was filled with fear. By the time I left, one year later, I used a blanket at night because I was chilly. And I stayed above ground when the rockets hit.

Even walking point sometimes became routine, and the reality of danger gave way to daydreaming. Much like driving a car and being lost in thought, I occasionally forgot to be afraid.

And it was the same way with my shit-burning duty. At first, I hated it. Then I moved to, *I'm not going to let the first sergeant get the best of me!* Eventually, I became used to it and it didn't bother me anymore.

When you do something long enough, you become conditioned.

The Bad and Good of Adapting

While the ability to adapt to new conditions is good, it can work against you when you're trying to succeed.

Watch for becoming so conditioned to doing things in a certain way that it becomes routine. You won't realize that you're in danger. I'm not necessarily talking about physical danger, like in Vietnam. It could be financial danger. Maybe you waited too long to adjust your business plan and your company is failing. It could be emotional danger. Perhaps you think everything is okay in your family, but you aren't communicating with your spouse or your children and you're about to lose the relationships.

When I'm facilitating Life Success's Basic seminar each month, I meet countless people who defend their positions. And they're usually defending what isn't working in their lives! They're proud to defend their limitations.

People often tell me, "I have the right to be angry." Absolutely right! You do have the right to be angry. But does this get you what you want in your life? Most angry people want revenge. Have you ever tried to even a score through revenge? It really doesn't work for either person.

When people tell me about what's not working in their lives and I offer a suggested remedy, I usually am told, "But you don't understand!" They've adapted to being angry. Many people really don't want a solution. They'd have to change what they're doing. They'd have to be honest, which is dangerous to them. It doesn't feel safe.

The funny thing is that I do understand. I understand that once a person is conditioned, it's difficult for them to want to change. Most people change when where they are in life is more painful than the fear of change.

If you're like me, you're afraid of something every day. If I let fear control me, it's all over.

You can be afraid and have what you want. Or you can be afraid and not have what you want.

It's your choice.

The great thing about adapting is that you can weather storms. In the recent recession, lots of companies changed. Some competitors even worked together to survive in the new business environment, doing what they would've considered dangerous a few years ago. They adapted to the marketplace and found their way through the mess. Companies failed if they didn't—or wouldn't—change.

Remember I was the one who said I'd never sleep in the barracks during rocket attacks: *I will never be like those idiots!* And soon enough, I was one of the idiots.

Never say never.

Life is always changing, so it makes sense that we need to keep adapting and changing with life.

Danger is found in routine. This danger shows up as lack of commitment, character, or integrity—and the cause of a slow death.

Back In the Field

After my first time patrolling with Squanto and a few days back in base camp, it was time for me to go into the field with Chico. Another scout-dog handler with in-country experience would observe me this time out.

I was really nervous, thinking about all I needed to remember. I was afraid of what I didn't know. We practiced simulated Vietnam conditions during my training, but this was completely different. It doesn't matter how much you practice with fake bullets. When you get to the real thing, it's totally different! And I was really nervous about how the company I was about to work with would feel about a new guy walking point for them.

Reality was settling in—Chico and I had only had a short time to work together. I hoped that nothing happened while we were on patrol so I'd have enough time to learn his style.

Just like humans, each dog has his own personality. Chico and I needed to spend some time together to get used to working as a team.

My greatest challenge was becoming familiar with Chico's style of alerting. When I worked with Rommel at Fort Benning, we were together for three months. I knew how to read his alerts, and I knew exactly what was happening.

If we encountered the enemy, I was confident that I'd be able to read Chico's alert. My main concern was Chico's ability to sense tripwires and my ability to recognize those alerts.

The second challenge with Chico was that he was still a little aggressive with me. I knew that if anyone else came too close to him, he would surely bite. I could warn people about Chico, but he was good at drawing people in and quickly turning on them. I didn't want to work with troops who were angry with me because my dog bit them!

Bottom line: I had many thoughts, and they all scared me. All of my fears were upon me.

During those first five days on patrol with Chico, I learned a few things about handling him as we got on and off the choppers. As I said earlier, eagle flights were very challenging because so much was going on at one time.

But I found that if I was the first soldier on and off the chopper, I could keep Chico on a short leash and had a better chance of him not biting anyone. Once I was on the helicopter, I could hold Chico by his choke collar and he behaved.

Chico and I had come a long way together. In a short time, he'd moved from biting me to taking commands.

I was really excited to be on my way to understanding my job as point man. And I was looking forward to getting over my initial fear of the unknown—being in the field, walking patrol, and working with Chico. Chico was a good dog, and, with each day, the question, "Am I safe?" seemed to be less on my mind.

Before I knew it, my first time in the field with Chico had ended. And the first week was exactly what I wished for. I had the opportunity to work with Chico without running into any enemy action. Added bonus: Chico behaved, and we made it through the first week in the field without him biting anyone!

I already had finished two weeks in the field. Only fifty more to go!

Familiar and Comfortable

I wanted to know Chico and understand his behavior so we could better work together. People are much the same way: I like to figure out how I can better understand and work with them.

Life Success Seminars has a nine-member board of trustees. Each year, a few board positions are open for election. When new board members are elected, I'm excited to hear new perspectives from new people. But after more than sixteen years, I've come to expect something different.

What generally happens is that the new members usually say something like, "I just want to observe for a while to see how the board works. I don't want to step on any toes." Or maybe they're really saying that working with seasoned members is just like working with Chico—they may bite!

"Playing it safe" is common for most people as they face new situations. They want to size up the situation and decide how they fit inside the current space. The new kid on the block usually looks for permission from inside the existing organization. Very few individuals enter and carve out their special spot—inserting their position instead of filling a position. The latter is less risky.

Most people gravitate toward what is familiar and comfortable. The problem with doing what's comfortable is that you usually don't generate many new and creative ideas.

This seems to be life's big joke: Life is always changing and that's scary, so people avoid change. Instead of change, people seek comfort and what's familiar. In the end, they're bored because the familiar isn't exciting.

When I first started as executive director of Life Success, I needed the board to give direction and help with decisions until I better understood operating a nonprofit. The longer I was in my position, the more I made decisions on my own.

About a year and a half after I started, the president of the board said she was concerned because I was making a lot of "I" statements about decision-making instead of "we" statements. She wasn't happy with my response when I told her that "I" was hired to run the company and I was ready to do that!

I understood how she felt, because I had changed. I needed help to get started, but as I got stronger in my job, I was the one who needed to make the decisions. My job is to report to the board—not necessarily to fit in with them.

The reality is that life is just one big learning curve, and you decide where you want to jump in or check out. We all have to ask ourselves the question, "Where am I needlessly playing it safe?" Are you holding back in your relationships, your career, and even with yourself? Are you being honest?

How many times do you sacrifice a great idea because you want to play it safe?

Comfort = moderate joy. Familiar is boring!

Going to the Mountaintop

Approximately twenty-five scout-dog teams were assigned to the Forty-sixth Scout Dog Platoon. Each handler took a turn in the rotation; when it was your turn, you'd go into the field. We supported the Twenty-fifth Infantry Division, and any of the units within the division could request a scout-dog team.

As I said before, a scout-dog team would go into the field for five days and then return to base camp for a few days. But there was one exception to the five-day rule.

Our platoon supplied a dog team for a base camp on top of Nui Ba Den, a mountain close to Tay Ninh. Every ten days, a helicopter flight delivered supplies to the base. The flight also transported soldiers on or off the mountain. Our platoon had a scout-dog team on the mountain at all times, so scout-dog teams would rotate every ten days.

The rumor was that the US controlled the top and bottom of the mountain and that the VC controlled the rest of Nui Ba Den. We heard that the mountain was riddled with tunnels and that the VC had an underground hospital in the mountain. I'm not sure what was rumor and what was fact.

When we went to the camp at the top of Nui Ba Den, Chico and I patrolled the inside perimeter at night and I called in alerts. I was only at the mountaintop camp once, and it was a gravy job. Working at night on top of a mountain meant the temperature was cool, which was a nice break from patrolling in the heat of the day. And it was safe inside the perimeter of the camp.

Walking patrol on the mountain was useless because the wind gusted so hard that if Chico gave an alert, he could've been sensing danger from Chicago! Each night, the guys on duty with me would ask me to call in an alert, just for kicks, so we could watch a great light show. After I called in an alert, the choppers arrived and began to fire on the mountain right below us. The view of the combat activity lighting the night was amazing.

One night when I called in an alert, an old World War II–type plane showed up and put on an awesome display of night firepower. I'm sure it was even better for some of the guys who smoked weed!

This was the job I thought I'd have when I first heard that I was going to be a scout-dog handler. I got what I expected—but only for a week and a half.

Working the top of the mountain was one of the few times that it was fun to be a scout-dog handler. For a ten-day period, I felt safe.

Over the Top

Several years ago, two of my buddies invited themselves to exercise with me. I'd read the book *Fit for Life* by Harvey and Marilyn Diamond, and my kids had challenged me to get in shape. I'd been working out in my basement for a year before Dan and Tony joined in.

Our workouts soon added another element, which was challenging each other to set big personal goals. Dan wrote "14er" on the large dry-erase board hanging in my basement. Since Tony and I didn't know what a 14er was, Dan explained that this was the name for a 14,000 foot mountain. And he said that we would all go to Colorado and climb one.

I had no idea what I was getting into.

When we arrived in Colorado later that year, I thought Dan was kidding when I first saw what looked like mountains to me. He called them foothills.

Tony kept telling me that we really weren't going to climb a mountain. He figured that Dan would take us golfing. I hoped Tony was right, because I didn't think I was up to a 14er. I didn't feel so fit for life!

We spent the night at Dan's condo in Beaver Creek. That should've been my first clue that I was in over my head. About every half hour, I woke up because I was having a hard time breathing. What else did I need to know beyond the fact that I couldn't breathe while resting at 8,000 feet?

But at 5:45 the next morning, we stood at a footpath on Mount Elbert, the highest mountain in Colorado. We were at 10,000 feet, and I could barely breathe as we started to hike the mountain.

Five of us were on the climb—our friends Matthew and Don had come with us. Almost immediately, we started to separate because of fatigue. Tony became sick before the first bend in the trail, and he dropped behind. I stayed with Dan and the rest until we reached the tree line—where the trees stopped growing.

I'd wondered occasionally how good my heart was, and I figured this was the test that would show if I had any problems. As we hiked, I would take two steps and have to stop. I could see my heart pounding through my shirt.

I'd never experienced cardio activity like this.

By 2 p.m., I was at 13,000-plus feet and became as sick as a dog because of the altitude. I decided to turn around and head back. I was so exhausted and sick that my trip down the mountain to our starting point took three hours.

I was surprised at the amount of fear I experienced as I walked down the mountain. I didn't know if I could make it, and no one was with me.

I was alone.

Have you ever been in a position where you knew you bit off more than you could chew—and it's too late to do anything about it? Have you ever had the feeling of being in over your head and knowing you're alone on your journey? That is the moment you get to decide, "Do I sink or swim?"

Are you safe?

I was in bad shape, but I made it down the mountain.

It's funny the way life works. When I was on Nui Ba Den during the war, I felt safe. When I was on Mount Elbert, I felt unsafe.

A few years after our Colorado trip, I recorded a meditation CD entitled *The Mountaintop Centering*. The meditation is about breaking through self-imposed barriers to reach the mountaintop of your dreams—what you want in life. I included pictures of Nui Ba Den and

Mount Elbert on the CD cover because both mountains had a big impact on my life. But it was much easier to record the CD than to actually climb a mountain.

And I'm crystal clear that the only mountaintops I'll see in the future will be the ones in the recesses of my mind!

Being in over your head is okay. Just remember to come up for air now and then!

Rotating the Scout-Dog Teams

When I first joined my platoon, I made a countdown calendar so I could mark off each day that I was in Vietnam. The calendar started with 365 and went down to the day I would go home. I also kept a log of when I was in the field and what unit I worked with each time.

It didn't take long for me to see that the rotation schedule wasn't exactly fair. And the first sergeant—my good buddy—was the one responsible for creating the schedule. As a result of my conflict with him, not only was I on shit detail while in camp, but I also was sent to the field more often than I should've been.

Some guys were suck-ups, and they seemed to be passed over frequently in the rotation of the scout-dog teams. After three months of duty, I had more time in the field than some of the soldiers who had arrived in Vietnam three months earlier than me.

But the more I went into the field, the less I was afraid. I was getting used to my new environment. And I didn't have time to sit around and worry.

When we were in base camp, it seemed like the first sergeant was more interested in aggravating us than letting us rest. So when I was in from the field, I just kept my mouth shut and went about my business.

At one point, the first sergeant noticed that I kept a record of my activities in the field and questioned me about why I kept a log. I told him the truth—this was my way of keeping track of where I'd been and how much time I had left. He thought that my records were more sinister, and he kept questioning me.

I don't remember how it happened, but the conversation moved to rotation in the field. When I told him that I was moving though rotation faster than others, he denied manipulating the schedule.

At one point in the argument—just to get his goat—I thanked him for sending me out so often. I told him that he was doing me a favor. "If I'm going to get killed, I'd rather do it early in my tour," I said. "On the other hand, you'll be gone soon. I'll have the most days in the field, and I'll be the first to stop rotation and become a sergeant."

The rotation continued the way it always had, and that was fine with me. The more I went into the field with Chico, the safer I felt. I was in a routine and was more confident.

Eventually, the first sergeant's tour was over. I was happy to see him leave. We were assigned a new first sergeant—the one who was worried about fragging. The new first sergeant was as equally wacky as the previous one, just in a different way.

The benefits of being in the field so often did pay off when it was time for some of the guys to return home. I was pulled out of the rotation early and promoted to sergeant.

What started out looking like an injustice ended up being a blessing to me in many ways. Although I began to feel unsafe again toward the end of my tour, the reality is that life in base camp was a lot safer than walking point.

Life's Not Fair

As I went into the field so often, I remember thinking, *This isn't fair!* If you're like me, it's easy to fall into a trap, thinking that life should be fair.

When I worked as a pipefitter, I was laid off frequently. When I wasn't working, I remember my five kids wanted things that I couldn't afford. One year at Christmas, Cabbage Patch Kids were the hot item, and my youngest daughter, Coleen, wanted one. I knew we couldn't afford to buy one. And I felt like it wasn't fair.

The week before Christmas, my older brother asked me to follow him to a garage in Kentucky so he could drop off his car for repair. On the way back, we stopped at a little country store to buy soft drinks. When I paid for my drink, the woman who waited on me asked if I wanted to buy a $1 chance on a Cabbage Patch doll. I thought, *What the heck?* I bought one chance.

When we left the store, I didn't give it much thought. On December 23rd, the call came: I won the doll! The store was closing early for Christmas, so Nancy and I rushed. It was snowing, and I was afraid we wouldn't get there in time. But we did.

Tears still come to my eyes as I remember my little girl's face when she first saw her doll.

I was always afraid that my kids would be disappointed in me because of the struggles we had as a family. I often felt like a total failure as a dad because I couldn't give my kids the things that they wanted and needed.

When I won the doll for Coleen, I didn't feel like a failure.

How often do you think that life's not fair? Do you ever feel like you aren't getting your fair share? Do you think other people have too much?

Actually, life *is* fair. We all have good luck and bad luck.

Who was the first person to come up with the idea that life should be fair?

Life isn't fair, so share a few of your blessings with others to even it up.

Walking Point

When I walked point, I gave instructions to the company's leaders about what to expect from me as far as giving signals. I let them know that if my dog alerted, I may stop and kneel or I might hit the ground quickly. It all depended on what Chico did.

And I gave instructions about what I needed from the unit in the way of support. I wanted two guys with me—one on my right side and one on my left. I wanted the rest of the company to follow right behind us. I wanted them close for safety reasons. My focus was on Chico. If he missed an alert, the troops were my backup.

In addition to working with a variety of units, I worked in many different types of terrain. Most of the time, I patrolled in jungles, rubber tree plantations, and rice paddies. Working in rice paddies definitely had its challenges. I was in full view in open terrain, and I needed to pay extra attention to the dikes—ditches—in the paddies.

I noticed the same pattern with almost every company that I worked with.

In open terrain, the units followed my instructions and stayed close behind me. But when the terrain changed and we approached the jungle, the men would always drop back—leaving a big gap between us.

When this first happened, I became really angry. I felt as if they were using me as a guinea pig. Here I was in a war, working with people who really didn't know me. I was walking point for them, and I felt unsafe.

When I looked around and saw that the unit had fallen back, I knelt down to wait for them to catch up with me. Besides, I was tired. What I forgot was that I had told them that my kneeling meant that Chico was alerting, so they all hit the ground. It actually was pretty funny for me, but not so much for them!

Eventually, I figured out that the units were going to drop back often, and it was my responsibility to make sure the company was right behind me. I learned to check on the troops more often and keep them close behind Chico and me.

We all were afraid of walking up to a wood line—we didn't know who might be waiting for us. But they didn't trust Chico like I did.

As the months passed by, Chico and I had become a great team. Chico actually was the perfect dog for me. He had an attitude, just like I did!

Leading Your Team

The only way life works is if you own it. You're responsible for your part. And you're responsible for leading those around you.

If a situation feels dangerous, it's the same as walking up to a wood line while on patrol. The team will drop back because they're afraid.

As a leader—and we're all leading someone—you must remember that *you* are the point person. Remind those around you that you're in the lead, you'll keep them informed, and you have the situation under control.

Just as I kept the troops close to me, you have to keep your team close.

When revenue is down, managers can expect the team to drop back because people don't feel safe. Think about it: Staff cutbacks, wage reductions, or a host of other issues could affect their future. As a business leader, this is important to realize. When fear looms, stop often and communicate with your support troops.

Good leaders work with their team to limit unnecessary fear and stress. And your team isn't just the people at work—your family and friends are part of your team.

Remember that every position is critical. If everyone on the team—whether it's at work or at home—doesn't own their positions, the mission is in jeopardy.

While the point position—the leader—has an important role, you're in a dangerous position if you're not backed by support.

And when you don't feel safe, you need courage to push forward.

"Owning it" means taking personal responsibility. Lead. Take the point position in your life.

Off the Boat

For one week, I was stationed in the Delta. We were taken by boat each day to a predetermined location to begin our patrol.

The platoon leader told me that on this day, we'd be dropped off in an area where the water was five-feet deep. He said that we only had to walk a short distance and we'd be on dry ground.

As a scout-dog handler, I could opt out of situations where I felt that Chico couldn't work properly. My judgment told me not to go on the patrol and just stay on the boat, but we went anyway.

When we arrived at our destination, I jumped off the boat. The water was shoulder high. I pulled Chico by his leash into the water, and he began to swim. I was trying to keep my M16 over my head so it wouldn't malfunction if I needed it later.

I don't know how to swim, and I could feel panic about to take over. I was afraid that there'd be a spot where the terrain dropped off. Since I was in full gear, like a human anchor, I figured that I'd drop off, too!

It was tough enough to walk wearing my boots and clothes. But the water level didn't seem to be changing, and Chico was getting tired. I knew I needed to do something quickly.

I slung my rifle over my shoulder, grabbed Chico and put him on my shoulders. I was exhausted. Trying to keep Chico out of the water was almost impossible. He was frantic and scrambling to stay safe.

The longer we walked, the more my fear grew. I'd felt that we shouldn't get off the boat. I'd known that this was a disaster waiting to happen, but I didn't follow my gut.

I finally stopped and asked the platoon leader why we hadn't reached land yet. I was amazed at what I heard next! "They just radioed me that they dropped us in the wrong place," he said. "We need to go back to meet the boat."

I didn't know if I was more afraid or angry at this point!

I wasn't sure that I could make it back to the boat. I was exhausted, and Chico was in a panic. Each time I made him swim so I could rest, he became frantic and tried to climb back on my shoulders.

Eventually, we made it to the boat and were safely on deck. But my feeling of relief went away quickly.

I noticed that Chico was covered with leaches. As bad as that seemed, I quickly realized that all of the soldiers were covered with leaches, too. I was truly amazed that I could have that many leaches on me. And I didn't have a clue about how to remove them.

What an experience that was! After walking neck-deep in water to the point of total exhaustion, I stripped naked with fifty other guys so we could check each other for leaches in places you can't see on yourself.

But I was glad to find out that getting rid of leaches is pretty simple. The leaches fell off when we sprayed them with bottles of Army–issue insect repellent.

I'd never seen a leach before that day, and I knew I never wanted to see one again. They are gross!

Trusting Your Gut

've experienced many times when I didn't trust my gut, listened to the advice of others—and regretted it later.

When you're in a leadership position, it's really important to have good people around you who can give you advice when making decisions. What you have to watch is that good people with good intentions can sometimes give bad advice.

I've been the leader of a nonprofit for more than sixteen years, and I still fall into this trap. Some very high-powered, successful businesspeople are members of Life Success's board of trustees. I sometimes think that they know more than me. The reality is that in many areas, they do have good ideas and can help Life Success perform better. But in other areas, my gut is more accurate.

If anyone knows the organization, it's me. After all, I'm running it day in, day out.

I've listened to advice that our nonprofit is just like any other business. I've hired highly qualified people, but they weren't passionate about our mission of putting people first. So they didn't do their jobs with passion.

Just like my gut told me to stay on the boat, I knew they weren't the right people to hire. But I didn't trust myself, and I made the wrong decisions.

Do you remember when I mentioned earlier in the book that I trusted my gut and quit a job, which turned out to be political suicide in the pipefitters union? Let's look at that decision from a long-term perspective.

Had I stayed on the job and later won the business-agent election, I would've remained a pipefitter. And I probably would've retired after working another twenty years in a career I didn't like.

Because I quit the job and lost the election, I had to make decisions. I knew I wanted to be a leader, and this forced me to make different decisions that ultimately led me away from pipefitting to becoming the leader of Life Success.

My volunteer leadership positions at Life Success began a whole new direction in my life. I eventually became head of the organization. This role opened the door to my facilitating seminars and workshops. And that led me to writing books and speaking to thousands of people.

The challenge for me is to stay aware. Other people have good ideas, but so do I. I'm the executive director of Life Success because I have the ability to make good decisions. I must stay clear in order to recognize what is good advice and when I should trust my gut.

How much time do you spend developing your intuition? If you're like most people, you've spent a lot of time and money developing your knowledge. But how much have you spent on gut work—on developing your intuition and your emotional well-being?

Decisions usually are based on emotions, so you can expect disaster if you're immature in that area. You're only as good as the applications you have available. It's important to slow the decision-making process so you can separate your ego from your gut.

When you don't feel safe, you make defensive decisions. When you don't feel safe, it's hard to be creative. When you don't feel safe, you don't trust yourself.

When you don't trust your gut, you end up with stomach problems!

The Perfect Landing

During monsoon season, life in Vietnam was pretty wet. Staying dry was hard, and wet boots and fatigues eventually take a toll. I had a lot of foot problems and rashes from being wet all the time. So I was excited when we patrolled on dry ground, which wasn't all that often.

On one assignment, our eagle flight was coming in to the most beautiful green area I'd ever seen. Nothing to fear here—we would patrol in open terrain and dry, green fields.

After being in Vietnam for a while, I was pretty comfortable with eagle flights even though I never knew what to expect on drop-offs or pickups. Once I was on the chopper, I sat in the doorway and held Chico by his choke collar. A six-foot leash was hooked to his collar, and the strap at the other end of the leash was around my wrist.

When I jumped, I released Chico so he could run for six feet after hitting the ground. I needed those seconds to adjust my gear—my backpack loaded with our supplies for the week, including food, water, and ammunition—before being pulled forward by Chico. I also carried my M16 and wore a steel pot (helmet) on my head.

On this day, the chopper came in and hovered about three feet off the ground. When we got the signal to go, I jumped. What came next was one of those great surprises that you often get in life.

I released Chico as I hit the ground, like I always did. But this time was a little different. I sunk to my knees in mud.

I immediately came to a dead stop, but Chico was much lighter and had four legs, so he kept moving forward.

As Chico ran, he pulled me forward because the leash was secured around my wrist and I couldn't let go quickly enough. I heard and felt the suction of the mud on my legs, and I began to fall forward. For a moment, I thought I might recover—my rifle stuck upright in the mud and slowed my fall.

But Chico was still on the move.

The next thing that happened was unbelievable. My steel pot fell off my head and landed with the open end up. I continued to fall—without the use of my hands—and I landed face first in my helmet. I thought for sure that I'd broken my nose, neck, and both legs, but I didn't have a scratch on me.

I must've looked absolutely ridiculous. If I had a video of this, it would get a million hits on YouTube!

This is what I learned that day: Life is always full of surprises!

Just because it looks all clear, you might not be safe.

The Grass Is Always Greener

Part of being a leader—whether you're an entrepreneur, managing a company, or raising a family—is that you have to assess the situation and make decisions. Just like the green and perfect-looking landing field, many things aren't what they seem.

It's easy to look at other people and think that they have it all figured out. When you aren't with someone on the journey but only see the fruits of their work, it's easy to think that they're just lucky.

I have a good friend who is really successful. He has it all—a really nice house, a couple of vacation homes, multiple Mercedes, and plenty of money to spend. He belongs to country clubs at home and where he vacations. You know this kind of guy, right? He's the lucky one!

We've been friends for more than twenty years and, in the beginning, I was jealous. I didn't think it was fair that he was so lucky. The longer we were friends, the less I was jealous. Now I actually thank God that I'm not him. I think he's a great guy—he's the best. But I don't want to be him because I see the price he has paid—and continues to pay—for his success.

It's easy to think the rest of the world is getting a break and you're not. It's easy to think that other people are lucky for the end rewards they have without looking at their hard work and sacrifices. It's easy to go beyond jealous and believe that they should give you part of what they have. After all, they have plenty!

Success has a price, and you have to be willing to pay the price to succeed. Are you willing to work eighty-plus hours a week to get your business up and running? Are you willing to have your family be without you because you're too busy at work? Are you willing to sacrifice a high-powered career so you can spend time with your family and friends?

I've been told many times that I am lucky. I think I'm blessed more than lucky. I'm not a quitter, and it's hard to beat someone who doesn't quit.

When I ask people why they think I have my job as executive director of Life Success, they usually answer, "Because you love it." I do love what I do, but the real reason I have my job is that I wouldn't quit. I volunteered for countless hours and learned about the organization.

I was willing to do what was needed, even when it didn't feel safe or fair.

When I first volunteered at Life Success, I wanted an ovation—just like everyone else. I spent a lot of time being jealous of other people when I thought they were getting ahead of me.

Somewhere along the line, I figured out that jealousy was just lack of vision on my part. When I felt underappreciated, I didn't go away like a lot of the people who said they wanted the same things I wanted. I was told "no" often, but I refused to accept "no" for an answer.

When I lack clarity for my future, I want what someone else has. When I'm clear about my vision, I'm grateful for my life.

Instead of being jealous of someone else's success, how do you create a plan for taking action in the direction of your dreams? When you're willing to sacrifice your safety for courage and action, you will succeed.

I guarantee that when you have a vision and are committed to an action plan, you'll come to a place where people say *you* are the lucky one!

Even when the grass looks greener for others, remember that your growing season will produce greener grass in the near future.

Am I Safe?

When I arrived in Vietnam, I didn't feel safe. But the longer I was there, the more my feelings changed. I eventually felt safe when I was in base camp. And I ended up trusting Chico so much that I often wasn't afraid when I walked point.

When people are familiar with their surroundings and with their actions, they feel comfortable or safe. They adapt. They're conditioned.

If you're facing the unknown and you're afraid, it's tough to feel safe. But you aren't necessarily unsafe just because you're afraid.

Of course, I'm not talking about physical danger. We're looking at the confusion between "being unsafe" and "fear." Ask yourself this question: "Is this decision going to injure or kill me?" If the answer is "no," you're probably safe.

Each time you take your business or your relationships to a new level, you can expect to face the challenge of trusting yourself even when it doesn't feel safe. It may or may not be a good decision, but it's not about safety.

It's about fear.

Should you take a risk with a new product line? You may not feel safe, but you're not in danger. In relationships, are you afraid to open your heart? You may be fearful of the risk, but you're safe.

Fear is a feeling, and everyone experiences fear. You're always going to be afraid—it's part of life. You can be afraid and have you want, or you can be afraid and not have what you want. Either way, you're going to be afraid.

I've watched too many people give up on their dreams because of fear. And they think that they aren't safe because of their feelings.

When are you going to start living your life, even if you're afraid? If you found out you were going to die today, what's on your list of regrets? That list is the beginning of your action plan.

Imagine a life lived in fear, one of being afraid to do what you're here to do. Would you be proud to have this on your tombstone?

**JOHN DOE LIVED HIS ENTIRE LIFE SAFELY,
AND HIS DREAMS DIED.
JANE DOE LIVED HER ENTIRE LIFE SAFELY,
AND HER DREAMS DIED.**

**BORN: 1950
DIED: 1995
BURIED: 2015**

**HERE LIE JOHN AND JANE DOE,
BURIED WITH THE DREAMS THEY TRADED
FOR A LIFETIME OF SAFETY!**

Safety is like a parachute—it's a backup, not a guarantee. Jump anyway!

Am I Alone?

Do you remember the three questions that I asked myself while I was in Vietnam—and that I still ask myself every day?

1. Am I prepared?
2. Am I safe?
3. Am I alone?

While I was in Vietnam, my answer to the third question was, "I sure feel alone!"

I had many reasons to feel alone from the minute I landed in Vietnam. Like most guys in the war, I was drafted at a young age, had never been away from home, and didn't have much experience with life. I faced many situations that I struggled with.

I've shared many examples of when I felt alone in Vietnam. I was walking point with a dog that didn't like me. That certainly made me doubt that I'd make it home safely! And I felt like the Lone Ranger since I constantly worked with different companies, not knowing anyone for more than five days. Walking point set me apart from the rest of the troops.

But was I really alone? Or was I lonely?

By this point in the book, you're probably cluing in that your actions aren't dictated by your feelings. While you may feel like you're alone, the reality is that you probably have good people around you who would help you, if you just asked.

Being alone isn't the same as being lonely. I meet people all the time who are lonely but are surrounded by people. Leaders who tell you that it's lonely at the top probably aren't telling you that it doesn't have to be that way. If you're lonely at the top, my guess is that you have issues with trust or intimacy—or both.

When you feel as if you're alone, ask yourself, "Do I have anyone who cares about me? Would they help me if I asked?" And if you don't like to feel alone, ask yourself, "Why do I feel uncomfortable by myself?"

When was the last time you sat by yourself and looked at your life? Why do you stay busy all the time?

It's okay to feel alone. It's okay to be alone.

We live in a fast-paced world, and it's really easy to rush through life only to find that you're alone because you didn't have time for relationships. At that point, you may be alone but you can choose to get back on track.

Most people feel unique and different in their problems but common or ordinary in whom they are. It's usually just the opposite—you're a unique person with common problems.

Whether you're alone or just feel alone, you have the ability to take action.

When you feel alone, is it true? Or do you use that feeling as an excuse to be aloof?

The Lone Ranger

After a long, hot day of patrolling, we arrived at a fire support base for the evening. A chopper arrived around 7 p.m. and brought cold beer for the troops. This didn't happen often, and I don't remember why beer was brought to this company.

But I do remember that the attitude in the camp immediately changed for the better. And it was apparent that I was on loan, that I wasn't one of them.

I wasn't offered a beer.

I felt unappreciated and betrayed. After all, I had just walked point for this company. I was risking my life for them, but I wasn't good enough to share a beer with. It sounds petty now, but, on that night, I felt like the loneliest guy on earth.

The sun was still out, and the heat was unbearable. The swarming mosquitoes looked big enough to suck a pint of my blood. I lay down on the ground and slid, on my back, into a small sandbagged shelter. I pulled my rain poncho over my head to keep the mosquitoes from biting me.

It was a defining moment. I wanted to give up. I was tired of being in Vietnam. I was tired of patrolling day after day and accomplishing nothing. I felt like nobody cared about me. I felt hopeless and lonely.

Why bother? I thought. *Am I really going to make it through all this and survive to go home?*

It was the loneliest moment of my life.

I really was like the Lone Ranger, out on my own. As I lay in the shelter with Chico at my feet, it was fitting that we were together. He fought life. He was a loner.

My bond with Chico was stronger from that point forward. He was a one-man dog—and I was his man. Chico and I were a team. In my opinion, we were the best scout-dog team in Vietnam.

The longer I was in Vietnam, the more independent I became.

Eventually, I didn't make much of an effort to get to know the people I worked with when I was on patrol. I figured that I was the hired gun, so it was better that I walk point rather than someone they knew and cared about.

Oddly enough, I began to feel safer and less alone because I now was 100 percent committed to Chico and me as a team!

The Buck Stops Here

Over the years, I've noticed a pattern to my behavior. I've always felt like I was different—a loner. I'm often with people yet feel alone, like walking point with a platoon of soldiers who don't know or care about me.

As a young boy, I thought I couldn't depend on the people who were the authority—my parents. My dad was an alcoholic and didn't command respect or have the ability to influence people. My mom was a good woman who spent her whole life trying to hold things together and keep food on the table.

But I didn't trust that they were going to take care of me. I figured that I had to rely on me and me alone.

In my mind, this translated into the idea that if I'm in charge of me, there wasn't much room for someone else to tell me what to do. I knew from an early age that I was going to take care of all of my needs so I could avoid relying on others. So what if the platoon didn't offer me a beer? When my time came, I'd buy my own.

I wouldn't depend on anyone. I'd take care of myself.

That didn't always work so well.

Like my original relationship with Chico, I've been 99 percent committed many times in my life. I always left myself a trap door—or an escape hatch—from responsibility. One of the ways I can tell that the buck isn't stopping with me is when I think, "Life isn't fair."

When I'm afraid, feeling unsafe and alone, I play the blame game.

For most of my life, I thought that 99 percent effort was something to be proud of. After all, it was almost 100 percent. Looking back, I can see the places in my life where that 1 percent could've made the difference between triumph and disaster. Many things have become clear to me during the past twenty-five years, and the importance of 100 percent commitment is one of those things.

Nancy and I have been married for more than twenty-five years, and we've had many struggles to resolve. Our five kids are pulled in many directions, so we focus our attention on finding solutions to our blended family.

A few years ago, Nancy had brain surgery. The results of the operation left her worse than before. She's now in a lot of pain and can't predict how she will feel from moment to moment, so it's hard for us to plan anything.

But we are 100 percent committed to the relationship. The buck stops with us.

I don't believe that you can maintain total personal responsibility when you aren't focused. That's why each of us needs to be clear about who and what we're committed to.

What has the buck stopping at your door?

I'm committed to do whatever it takes to succeed in the three main areas of my life: Nancy, our five children, and the future of Life Success. If I do a good job in those three areas, I'll have lived a wonderful life!

Have you ever stopped and made a list of your buck-stops-here areas? Doing this will clear up a lot of responsibility issues and your fear of potential outcomes. Fear and loneliness are amplified when you don't trust others. Knowing who is responsible for what will be critical to your success.

"The buck stops here" is a commitment to personal responsibility.

You Can't Pin a Medal on Chico

C hico was an amazing dog. While it took some time for us to work things out, Chico really was a one-man dog. It's amazing that we came together at all—we both were loners who didn't trust. But we ended up as a team.

Chico was very protective of me and would bite if anyone startled him or got in our space. In the end, we really weren't alone.

We had each other.

When I was in base camp with my platoon, I did a little research and found out about Chico's history. I wrote his civilian owner, a police officer in North Dakota, and sent him pictures of Chico in Vietnam. We exchanged letters and Christmas cards for years.

Chico's owner donated him to the Army because Chico, in a misguided attempt to protect the man's small daughter, had jumped through the screen door and bit the mailman. As a result of me sending his owner some photos, Chico was featured in his hometown paper.

After learning about Chico's history, I realized that I was just one in a long line of people whom Chico had bitten!

One day while on patrol, we were walking a wide path used by tanks and armored personnel carriers, which transported troops. The path wasn't used often, but it was still passable and clear of trees. As we walked the trail, Chico alerted—but it was an odd alert. I stopped the patrol, and the patrol leader came up to talk with me.

I told him that Chico had alerted, but it was strange. Chico sensed a faint alert, which would indicate someone in the distance. But the terrain wasn't right for an alert at that distance, and the wind wasn't moving at the time of his alert. I concluded that we were right on top of something, but I didn't know what.

Once Chico gave an alert, my work was finished until everything was checked and determined to be all clear. The platoon leader called two soldiers to join us so I could explain what was happening. These two guys were going to check the trail in front of us. I told them that they needed to be very careful because of the possibility that we were close to a booby trap or something else.

The two soldiers moved forward with caution. About fifteen feet ahead, they found a tripwire across the path that was set to trigger explosives on both sides of the trail. Had I walked a little farther, we would've tripped the explosives. Many of us would've been badly injured or killed. The explosives were detonated, and no one was hurt.

The reason Chico's alert was so weak was that he was alerting on the smell left behind by the Viet Cong on the explosives. It's hard to believe that Chico could smell that scent, but he did. To this day, I think something special happened in that moment because Chico's alert was one I easily could've dismissed as nothing.

As a result of Chico's alert, I received my second Army Commendation Medal; this one came with a "V," for valor. The Army couldn't pin a medal on Chico, so he received a big steak once we returned to the Forty-sixth Scout Dog Platoon. And we were featured in the Twenty-fifth Infantry Division's newspaper, *Tropic Lightning News*.

Honestly, I would've been happier if Chico received the medal and I ate the T-bone steak!

I often felt alone and unappreciated many days while I walked point. But sometimes I felt as if I wasn't alone and had a good team behind me, like on this patrol.

Following Your Gut

Even though Chico's alert was different, the unclear signal was true. In life, we often receive signals that we don't understand.

I bought an English setter for my wife, Nancy, right before she had brain surgery a few years ago. Belle was a puppy when I brought her home.

After we had Belle for about three weeks, she snapped into a strange behavior. When we let her outside, she crouched and moved like a cat. This was the beginning of Belle's obsession with hunting birds every waking moment.

Belle's sense of smell is as keen as Chico's was. Belle can smell where birds landed in our yard while she was inside. If you didn't know that Belle is wired for birds, she'd look absolutely crazy. I'm not saying that Belle doesn't look crazy, but at least there's a reason!

Like Belle, we're trained to understand signals. But if we can't understand the signals, what should we rely on to make decisions?

During the first part of our life, we go to school. We read books, listen to teachers, and memorize information. We learn and analyze a lot of facts. We spend a lot of time—and often pay a lot of tuition—to develop our minds. By examining a problem and looking at what caused the problem, we come up with the reason that things are the way they are. We learn to make decisions based on information and understanding.

We're invested in the "why" of what happens in life. We have a hard time with what can't be explained by facts.

I believe that we all have intuition, instincts that can't be explained. You may believe it's something else, but I know you've experienced a gut feeling that exactly forecast something that happened.

My personal belief is that God works through me when I get out of my own way.

When Chico alerted on the tripwire, something told me to pay attention. The alert didn't make much sense. If I'd tried to make sense of his alert, I would've continued walking and tripped the booby trap. Chico's weak alert saved my life and the lives of many other soldiers.

Follow your gut.

When I applied for the position of executive director at Life Success, the odds seemed stacked against me. Therapists, counselors, and successful businesspeople applied for the position. I felt as if everyone was more qualified than me and that I was all alone with my limited education. Nancy had worked for Life Success for four years, and I'd been volunteering the same amount of time.

I met with some board members who told me that they selected a business executive to fill the position. But they asked me to stay on as lead volunteer because they felt I was the heart of the nonprofit. I was really disappointed, but I handled myself professionally. I told the board that I would keep my volunteer commitment until the end of the year and would make my ultimate decision later.

What I didn't know was that the other half of the board met with Nancy to let her know that I didn't get the job. And they introduced her to her new boss. It didn't go well!

When Nancy expressed her disappointment that I wasn't hired as executive director, her new boss said, "You really didn't think that they'd give Mike this job, did you? He's just a pipefitter."

She said the wrong thing to Nancy! Nancy called the president of the board and gave her two-week notice.

Later at our house, Nancy and I sat in our hot tub and talked. Nancy asked if I was okay. I told her that I was excited about my future. "What do you mean?" she said.

"I truly believe that God has brought me to this place," I said, "and if this isn't it, He must have something big in mind for me!"

I knew in my heart that I was the right person to run Life Success.

My gut told me to continue doing what I always did as a volunteer and to have faith. Three days later, the board president called Nancy and asked her to reconsider quitting. She also asked Nancy to set up a meeting with me and two members of the board.

In the meeting, I learned that the board had reconsidered. They offered me the position as executive director. I accepted.

I could've reacted to any or all of the events during the process, but my intuition told me to take the high road. As a result, it all worked out as it was supposed to!

Most of us haven't spent much time or money on developing our intuition. That's one of the many tools we teach at Life Success. We help people find a way to trust their intuition along with trusting their intellect.

Thinking and feeling are different. We're given both so we can make balanced decisions.

If you live solely in either world, life doesn't work well. If you live your life in your head, you'll try to understand life while missing the experience. If you live only in your feelings, you risk being ungrounded and riding the roller coaster of life.

Life is to be lived in intellect and intuition, in head and heart. Balance improves results, whether you're talking about business or personal relationships.

You alone know your gut feelings. You're alone when you use your intuition. And that's okay.

When was the last time you were in an arena that strengthened your courage to trust your own unique guidance system?

Your ability to trust your gut is in direct relation to your willingness to be alone.

Caring Matters

During my tour in Vietnam, the command of the Forty-sixth Scout Dog Platoon changed hands. The first sergeant—my shit-detail buddy—left about six months after I arrived. As I mentioned earlier, I didn't miss him much!

The commander position also changed around the same time. I don't remember who was the officer-in-charge when I first arrived. But I do remember the officer who took over for the rest of my tour. He was a lieutenant who had short-man syndrome. He also had a bit of a drinking problem. I didn't have any room to judge him, but I did.

The lieutenant had a very big ego, and he fed this ego with the lives of the scout-dog handlers under his command. He spent a lot of nights at the officers' club, drinking and drumming up business for the scout-dog teams. He told us that he was going to set the record for the most scout-dog teams in the field in one year. And he followed that statement with his reason: He felt this would lead to his promotion to captain.

As a result of the lieutenant's actions, many from our platoon were sent to companies that didn't need a dog team. I'd sometimes be assigned to a mechanized unit, and I'd spend the whole week sitting along the side of the road, protecting it for convoys. A dog team was of no use, but at least it was an easy week for Chico and me.

The lieutenant was on a roll, and all of the scout-dog teams spent a lot of time in the field because he wanted to be promoted. Our platoon had a couple of new soldiers who replaced some guys who had gone home. One of the new soldiers had just finished college, and his school deferment had ended. He was drafted quickly after graduation and, like most of the scout-dog handlers, wasn't too happy to be in Vietnam.

I hadn't said much to this guy—I'd been in the field a lot and had missed him because of our rotation schedule. He had completed his first two sessions in the field—one where he watched an experienced scout-dog handler and one where another handler observed him. After supper one evening, we both were in the common area outside of the platoon's barracks. He prepared his gear for the next morning, when he would go on patrol on his own for the first time.

I struck up a conversation with him, and I asked how he felt about going on patrol the next day. "Are you nervous?" I asked. What he said next really upset me!

He said that he wasn't nervous. "If my dog alerts and I see it, that's fine," he said. "And if he alerts and I don't see it, that's fine, too."

"What are you talking about?" I asked. "Your life depends on your paying attention to your dog's alert!"

"I really don't care because I don't agree with this war," he said.

"Join the group! None of us want to be here, but we are," I said. "And you don't have the convenience of not caring about your dog alerting."

We talked for an hour. He wasn't going to change his opinion or his attitude.

He thought he was the only guy in Vietnam who felt alone in the war.

He had the same feeling I had when I first arrived in Vietnam. I thought that it was impossible to walk point for a year—with a dog that didn't like me—and survive. But I was smart enough to know that I needed to change my attitude if I was going to have any chance of making it through the year.

On the soldier's second day on patrol, he walked into an ambush. He, his dog, and three soldiers died that morning. I don't know whether his dog alerted and he missed it, but I believe his attitude contributed to his death.

The next day, the lieutenant told one of my buddies and me to go to the morgue and identify the young man's body. As the platoon leader, this was his responsibility—not ours.

I refused to go and my buddy did, too. The conversation escalated. I finally said what I needed to say to the lieutenant. I told him that if he was the big man sending us on patrol so he could look like a star, he was the one who could identify the body and live with the memory.

I wasn't going to have the image of the soldier's dead body stuck in my head.

I figured that I'd be demoted, but the lieutenant never did anything to us for refusing his order.

The soldier's death was a big lesson to me. No matter what the situation, I don't have the convenience of thinking I'm alone and not caring about the people who rely on me to do my job.

Responsibility

Responsibility is one of the topics covered in the Basic seminar I facilitate for Life Success. Responsibility sounds pretty simple—you are responsible for yourself and responsible to others. But it's not easy.

The lieutenant wasn't acting responsibly when he needlessly sent scout-dog teams on patrol. He was gambling lives so he could be promoted to captain. When the guy in our platoon was killed, the lieutenant wanted my buddy and me to identify the body. But that was the lieutenant's responsibility as the platoon leader.

It's easy to think that your actions aren't affecting anyone even though they absolutely are. My dad was an alcoholic, and he thought he was just drinking. He thought he was alone in what he did, but he impacted everyone in the family.

When I was old enough, I began to drink. And my drinking often got out-of-hand. But I justified my drinking. Even though I drank, I went to work and provided for my family. My dad didn't provide, so I was better than my dad. In my mind, that meant I could handle my drinking.

My drinking impacted my first marriage. In my second marriage, my drinking became a problem, too. Nancy wanted me to participate in the Basic seminar with the hope that I'd recognize my drinking was a problem and I'd quit.

I thought it was unfair that everyone focused on my drinking. After all, I was fine. I provided for my family.

I didn't think I had a problem.

Although I still drank after I attended Basic in 1987, I did give up drinking in July 1989. My last drink was the night before participating in Inter-Personal Intensive (IPI), a five-day overnight seminar hosted by Life Success.

I realized that I was acting irresponsibly, and my actions were affecting my family. I was selfish, and I wasn't thinking about the people who I cared about the most. Six months later, I quit smoking cigarettes.

People often are amazed to learn that I quit drinking and smoking, cold turkey. The reality is I decided that I wanted something better.

For me, it wasn't about giving up something—it was about gaining something. During the IPI seminar, I decided to be in charge of the quality of my life, to become responsible. In my mind, drinking and smoking didn't fit into a life of personal responsibility.

An addiction is the number-one relationship in the life of the person with the addiction. I didn't want drinking and smoking to be my top relationships.

Just like the lieutenant, I had shown the people around me that acting irresponsibly was okay. Like him, I was selfish. And my family, friends, and coworkers paid a price for my actions.

Irresponsibility is the same as stating, "I am alone and to hell with you!"

I decided that I wanted to be a leader, especially for my children. I wanted to quit preaching. I wanted to show them how I was changing my life. I knew that would influence them more than anything I said.

I decided to spend the rest of my life being the very best example I could be. And I have kept that promise.

Only when I lead by example can I truly say that I am responsible to my children and everyone else I come in contact with.

Saying that you are responsible for your irresponsible behavior doesn't make you a responsible person. It's just an admission of irresponsibility.

Controlling Kentucky

One of the scout-dog handlers was injured and returned home. We needed to take his dog back to the camp where everyone arrived in Vietnam—the same place I met up with Chico—so the dog could be paired with a new soldier. The dog's name was Kentucky, and, judging by his attitude, he could've been Chico's brother. Kentucky was a mean dog.

The lieutenant assigned a buddy and me to take Kentucky to the camp. Neither of us wanted to go into Kentucky's kennel in order to get the dog into a shipping cage.

Kentucky, like all of the dogs, was chained to a stake in a small area. Three-foot-high concrete walls separated the dogs from each other. A cage door was in front of each dog's space, with fencing in the rear and nothing on top. We decided to go over the top of Kentucky's kennel and use two hog catchers to secure and muzzle him so we could get him into the shipping cage. (Hog catchers are wire hoops that you tighten around an animal's neck in order to control it.)

We tried to snare Kentucky, but this plan wasn't as easy as it seemed—the dog was really angry. The lieutenant showed up and told us what sissies we were. Little Big Man went into action: "Give me his leash and choke collar! I'll show you boys how to do this."

The lieutenant was on his own—we stepped back as he walked into the cage with Kentucky. In two seconds, the lieutenant was on the ground and bleeding all over the place. Kentucky had bitten the lieutenant on his upper arm, pulled him to the ground, and then went for his leg, close to the lieutenant's groin.

My buddy and I immediately started yelling, and Kentucky backed off. We pulled the lieutenant out of the cage.

The lieutenant went to the hospital and needed a lot of stitches in his arm and leg. My buddy and I went back to plan A and used the hog catchers to control Kentucky. We muzzled him and got him into the shipping cage.

When we delivered Kentucky to the base, we were told to chain the dog in his new kennel and take off his muzzle. We chained him, hooked a six-foot leash to the front of his muzzle, stepped back, and jerked off the muzzle from a safe distance.

That was the last I saw of Kentucky—and the last time I saw the lieutenant in the dog kennels.

When you act like the Lone Ranger long enough, you may get your wish and put yourself in danger!

In Over Your Head

Have you ever met someone like the lieutenant? Maybe you work for someone who wants to look smarter or better than they really are. The people around that person often pay a price for that behavior.

If you're a good leader or work for one, you know that good leaders empower the people around them. They don't play the "I'll-do-it-alone" card. When you act like you know it all, you'll eventually find yourself in over your head. A good leader surrounds themselves with people who are smarter than they are, especially in the areas where the leader is weak.

Earlier I talked about vision and how leaders sometimes need to make it up, just like Squanto did with the cigarette pack. When you surround yourself with great people, they'll be excited to figure out the "how" of the vision.

Empower the people on your team. You won't feel alone, and they'll own the vision. When your team owns the vision, they'll go the distance with you.

If your success is at the expense of your team, they won't trust or respect you. Trust is critical for someone to follow you. I didn't trust the lieutenant because he only looked out for his interests—he didn't seem to care about the men under him.

You can't command respect. You may not tolerate disrespect, but that doesn't mean people respect you.

Many people who get in over their heads are those who want control. Here's a great saying about control: "If you need to control, you're probably out of control."

Control is about not trusting yourself. Most people who control say that they don't trust others. But they won't admit the truth—they really don't trust themselves. So they need to control everyone else.

Many entrepreneurs have a hard time letting go of control. After all, most of them went into business believing they could do the job better than the person they worked for. If business goes well, the company will grow and hire people. That's where the problems often begin.

The owner may try to cover all the bases because no one can do it as well as he or she can. The work must be done alone. Eventually, the entrepreneur can't do it all, and details start falling through the cracks. A decision has to be made: Are you going to be the visionary or are you going to be a worker?

This usually is a big struggle for the owner, and some type of business seminar or leadership coaching may be needed to assist the entrepreneur through the process of letting go of control. Don't panic! You maintain the lead and the vision, but you delegate the actions.

You're still in control, but it's controlling in a healthier way.

This concept is illustrated easily in sports. If a team has one star who refuses to be a team player, the athlete may have many individual records but the World Series or Super Bowl will be out of reach. A team of good players is better than having one great player.

If you can't keep the team together, you'll always feel as if you're in over your head.

What is the solution? According to Jim Collins's book *Good to Great*, good leaders must get the right people on the bus and then the team can go anywhere. If you're the right leader with the right people, you'll look forward to challenges as opportunities. If you and your team are prepared, you won't be overwhelmed.

Don't try to do it alone!

When you think you're alone, this becomes true. And you'll be in over your head.

Coming Off-Line

The big day finally came—I was taken off-line. I had gone on enough patrols, and I no longer went into the field with Chico. I was now the supply sergeant for the Forth-sixth Scout Dog Platoon.

I was in charge of our platoon's supplies, which would've fit inside a ten by ten foot container. I had to sign for everything that had ever been issued to our platoon, but most of the supplies no longer existed. Or we had surplus supplies that we didn't need, like stoves, because we had traded for something that we did need. It was an Army thing.

But it really didn't matter. As with most wars, we all knew that we would eventually pull out and leave everything there.

I'd just been promoted, and I had to make a big decision: Do I give shit detail to someone else? I decided that I didn't want to saddle another person with the job. After all, I was conditioned. So I continued to burn shit until the day I left Vietnam

But a funny thing happened to me when I was off-line and near the end of my tour. I became afraid again. I thought I'd feel safer, but it was just the opposite. I had made it for so long while walking point, but the end was now in sight. What if I got hit by one of those rockets coming into base camp at night?

The feeling was much like when I first arrived in Vietnam and thought the guys were crazy for ignoring the danger. I began to feel like our company clerk, the one who low-crawled—naked—across the gravel parking lot to the bunker during a rocket attack.

Two things will kill you in war: being too careless or being too careful. Both seem to work about the same. I decided that I needed to keep doing what I'd been doing all year. But I have to admit that I did visit the underground bunker a little more often than I had during the previous ten months!

Once I wasn't patrolling, my war experience really changed because I had the opportunity to have some fun with the other guys in my platoon. Because the first sergeant had "liked" me so much and sent me out on so many patrols, I was the first of the guys I arrived with to come off-line. But new soldiers joined our platoon, and the men I knew best finished patrolling shortly after I did.

During my final month in Vietnam, I didn't feel like the Lone Ranger. I felt like I belonged.

The hardest part of being off-line was watching the new guys rotating in and out of the field. I knew what they faced each time they went on patrol. And I remembered what it felt like to be really tired and come in from patrol only to have officers mess with you during your few days off. When the new soldiers were in base camp, the rest of us tried to cover a lot of the tasks so they could relax and take it easy.

A few weeks before my one-year anniversary in Vietnam, I received my orders: I would head home in one week.

I was prepared to go home. I would soon be safe and back with my friends and family.

My Vietnam experience was coming to a close.

Pass It On or Pass It Up

"**I** had it tough, so I'm going to make it tough on the next guy." How many times have you heard someone say something like that?

I once facilitated a one-day workshop for a group of third-year medical students. During the workshop, they talked about the first-year students and how they were going to haze them. I asked the group if they liked the way they'd been treated during their early days in medical school, and they said, "Definitely not!" But they had to put up with hazing in their first year, so they felt that the new students should have to do the same.

Because they had it hard, everyone should struggle. Pass it on.

Years ago, Les Crane released a song called, "Love (Children Learn What They Live)." In some cases, people do live what they learn. But in many cases, this isn't true.

In my seminars, I often work with people who choose to do something different. I meet many people who were mistreated by their moms and dads, but these people are wonderful parents to their own children.

All of us have the ability to choose our actions. We aren't robots, programmed to do a certain thing. Of course, the environment that you grew up in has an impact on how you make decisions. But your childhood doesn't determine your decisions.

You have a choice.

How would your life be different if your job was to make others' lives easier? And what if you didn't make their lives easier because they deserved it, but just because you wanted to?

I volunteer with a nonprofit organization that works with men who are trying to get off of drugs and alcohol. I periodically go to the center to talk about responsibility and how to succeed in life. I've met a lot of good guys in this program—everyday Joes, college graduates, and doctors.

I met a guy who I thought was special, so I gave him the opportunity to attend the seminars at Life Success. As he progressed, I offered him a job at our conference center. He was a fabulous employee, and I was excited. But after a few months, he used his paycheck to buy drugs.

I was disappointed, but, after he resurfaced, we worked our way to a new agreement that he'd stop using drugs and would come to work every day. I really liked this guy and wanted to help him. He took three buses to get to work, so I bought him a car that cost $2000. To prove that I trusted him, I put the car title in his name. I told him that he could pay me back over time.

A few weeks later, I saw him for the last time. He spent his paycheck on drugs and sold the car for more drug money.

One of my employees said to me, "I bet that will be the last time you help anyone." I told her, "I sure hope not!"

I worked really hard to let go of the initial anger and betrayal that I felt. I knew I had to let go of my resentment because I wanted to be a giver. I remembered that he didn't ask for help. I offered to help because I thought it was the right thing to do.

Years later, the guy called me. He asked that I forgive him for what he had done. He felt bad about it. I told him, "Just like I can't make you feel bad, I also can't make you feel good."

This may sound like a word game, but it isn't. When I put down the situation, it became his to deal with.

He was alone with his guilt. I couldn't help.

I didn't have much most of my life, and I was always afraid that I might be selfish if I ever succeeded. But I choose to "pass it up" because I don't want to pass on needless difficulty. Just like burning shit, I see little value in watching someone else do something just to prove a point.

When I was growing up, some really good people helped me and showed me that they cared. I'd rather be like them.

Part of being a good leader, both at work and at home, is to empower others and to be a resource. Leadership is about lifting others up—not pushing them down. If you practice good leadership, you'll probably be taken advantage of at some point, but it's part of the leadership territory.

You decide. Pass it on or pass it up?

Givers gain, but it doesn't always feel good when you're giving.

The Sounds of Silence

One of my buddies and I arrived in Vietnam together, and now we headed to where we'd landed one year earlier. I was wired and couldn't sleep, so I was exhausted by the time we arrived at Bien Hoa Air Base.

The base had changed quite a bit. The terminal was now a block building, and the roads were blacktopped. I had the pleasure of using a flush toilet for the first time in a year!

After being processed, we waited to leave Vietnam. We gathered in a designated area to wait for our flight to arrive. I was outside smoking as our plane landed. We were instructed to board the plane once the new soldiers exited and the plane refueled.

The plane taxied close to the building, and the engines slowly went silent. The plane door opened, and the new soldiers stepped off.

As the soldiers waiting to go home, it was our turn to applaud. But the tradition must've been broken.

There was no ovation.

At this point, I'd been awake for two days and was dead on my feet. Once the plane refueled, I walked across the tarmac to the stairway leading to the door of the plane. I was finally going to step onto the plane that would take me back to "the world."

I was going home.

I walked up the steps and through the door of the plane. I couldn't believe it. It was surreal. As I took a seat, the troops chatted. Once everyone was on the plane, I heard the attendant close the door and lock it down.

I felt a chill run through my whole body, followed by a flash of goose bumps.

The plane taxied to the far end of the runway, turned around, and prepared for takeoff. It was early evening, and the sun was going down. The pilot announced that we were taking off, and the engines pushed us down the runway.

What happened next is something I will remember until the day I die.

When the plane lifted off, a brief cheer was immediately followed by dead silence. I can only speak for me, but the feeling wasn't so much that I was happy but that I was grateful and relieved.

I felt alone, as if I was the only one on the plane.

In my silence, all I could think about was how I felt a year earlier, which really seemed like five years ago. I thought about how I spent my first few days in Vietnam watching the two flights leave daily for the US. And I remembered thinking that I probably wouldn't make it home alive.

I'd made it.

But a year in Vietnam had taken its toll. I was tired. I was a different guy.

My view of life and of the world had changed dramatically. I was headed home to a country that seemed to be angry for peace. The country definitely wasn't supporting the war or the troops.

How would I go home and not talk about the biggest event in my life? What would I do with the feelings that changed how I viewed the world?

Once again, I was alone.

Am I Alone?

How many times have you felt like you were all alone in an important moment? Just like when I was in Vietnam, you can expect to feel alone if you're a leader. But that doesn't mean you really are alone.

Answering the question, "Am I alone?" is important for leaders.

When the time comes to make a decision that you're completely responsible for, it will be your choice alone. It's called personal responsibility. The buck stops with you.

When you're worried what others may think of you and your decisions, the feeling of "I'm alone" will surface. But no one can make decisions for you. Don't use your responsibility for making the decision as your reason not to seek advice.

Why would you try to figure out life on your own? It doesn't have to be lonely at the top. So many good people are out there, willing to help you. Great resources are available.

While you may feel like you're alone, you don't have to live that way.

Trust yourself. Surround yourself with good people so you aren't isolated. Learn to build a circle of influence that allows you to better live your legacy. Whether you end up using their advice or not, getting good input from a trusted circle is helpful as you make decisions.

Imagine that each day you spent time developing your relationship database. Find partners in the areas where you want better results. Develop a business plan for being a professional at living and improving the most important aspects of your life.

Imagine that you had a coach, advisor, or mentor in the seven most important areas of your life: health, finances, career, relationships, relaxation, spiritual well-being, and education. How would your life improve if you had a comprehensive plan and worked it each day? What if you had accountability partners?

This isn't as hard as it seems. As a matter of fact, your life will be simpler because you're not trying to do it alone!

When I have an important decision to make, I often go away. I take a long drive and listen to music I like. I need to be alone so I can make a clear decision.

Am I alone in these moments? Yes, but it's by design. Am I lonely? I don't have time to be lonely—I have too many good people in my circle of influence to feel lonely. I have people around me who care as much about my dreams as I do.

When you're 100 percent committed to your future, you'll see that you've never been alone. It's just that you haven't been showing up!

Am I prepared? Am I safe? Am I alone?

Challenge yourself to look for the answers to these three questions *after* you've taken action rather than before. Why? Life is about action—not answers.

Remember that being alone doesn't mean you have to be lonely.

Clarity

As our jet touched down and the captain turned off the air conditioning, I immediately felt the heat. An indescribable odor seeped into the plane.

The door of the plane opened as the engines went silent, and a set of stairs was pushed in place. As I stepped through the door, the heat almost knocked me over. It actually took my breath away.

I was really nervous as I walked down the stairway, and I could feel the tension in my body.

I took that final step onto the tarmac. I'd just entered a world that I'd dreaded for so long.

It was February 18, 2005. I was back in Vietnam.

I was at Bien Hoa, in the exact place where I arrived and departed from Vietnam during the war. Some of the old buildings were still standing, and, because of the quick way we pulled out of the war, some US equipment had been left behind.

As we walked toward the check-in area, I felt sick to my stomach. When we entered the terminal, my anxiety level ramped up. The customs agents were Vietnamese military.

The customs process was really slow, and it didn't help that locals cut in front of us. If we'd been in the US, I would've said something. But we were in Vietnam. Keeping my mouth shut seemed like the prudent thing to do.

Eventually, it was my turn. As the soldier silently looked though my passport, I couldn't help thinking, *What am I doing here?* The soldier finally stamped my passport, and I walked away with a sigh of relief.

In 2005, I knew it was time for me to return to Vietnam to complete the emotional process of dealing with the war. I wanted to replace the images of Vietnam in my head with more current images.

I had feelings stuck inside of me when I returned home from Vietnam in 1970, and I really wasn't sure what they were about. I didn't have clarity about my feelings until I returned to Vietnam in 2005.

My two trips to Vietnam, in 1969 and 2005, were taken thirty-six years apart and under vastly different circumstances. But both trips had a major impact on my life.

The American War

My good friend Ken organized our trip in 2005. Ken was a Vietnam veteran, and this was his second time back. Ken, four other US veterans, and my son Brad were with me on the trip.

We needed to meet our Vietnamese guide to start our ten-day trip, so we walked out of Bien Hoa airport into mass chaos.

This was the Vietnam I remembered—mopeds by the thousands, a sea of bright colors, the constant chatter of the crowd, and people persistently trying to get us to buy something. We located our guide and after a briefing on dos and don'ts, we went by van to our hotel.

The customs agents at the airport were very rigid, which scared me. But they really didn't represent the flavor of the people I came in contact with on my return to Vietnam.

During the war, it bothered me to see how some American soldiers treated the South Vietnamese. The people who cleaned our rooms, did our laundry, and polished our boots were nice. As a soldier, I always figured that the North Vietnamese guys fighting us were probably just like me—they didn't really know what the fight was about, either.

We all were just trying to get through the war alive.

When I went back to Vietnam, I was afraid of how the people would feel about Americans being in their country. After all, Americans still have a full range of viewpoints about the war and a lot of unresolved feelings.

I quickly realized that I could drop my guard a little because the Vietnamese seemed more intrigued by our size and body hair than hating us for being American. Most of the veterans on our trip were a tad overweight, and many Vietnamese would walk up to us, rub our bellies and laugh, saying, "Happy Buddha! Happy Buddha!" They also rubbed our arms because they were intrigued by the fact that Americans have so much arm hair.

What amazed me most about what they did was the fact that they were comfortable touching us. Just think how someone would react to you walking up to him and rubbing his belly in the US!

We got to know our guide pretty well during our ten-day trip. He'd been on the American side during the war. After the US pulled out, he was captured and spent two years in a reeducation camp. He told us that a few years after the war ended, the government allowed the people to own land and sell rice. Life changed. He said that after the Americans left, the government couldn't get the people to think the way they did prior to the war.

Our guide had sons in college, and we asked him how his sons felt about the war. His answer surprised me. He said that his sons tell him, "Get over it, Dad." The war isn't an issue in the lives of the next generation. When he shared what young Vietnamese think about "The American War," as the Vietnamese call it, I realized that Vietnam had moved on much better than we have in the US.

My son Brad was twenty-five at the time, and it was interesting to see Vietnam through his eyes. He didn't have any history with the country, so he moved more freely with the people than I did. I was more sensitive with Vietnamese my age than when I interacted with younger people, but I was still cautious. But Brad didn't worry whether or not they liked Americans.

Just like their next generation, my next generation—Brad—didn't know or care much about the war. Brad loved the people and said he'd like to visit Vietnam again.

That's when I figured out the emotions that were stuck inside of me.

Ever since I returned home in 1970, I'd felt badly about our role in the war. At age twenty-one, I could see the pain in people's eyes and, in my opinion, we were the reason for their pain. Right or wrong, that was the feeling I had.

I worried about them for thirty-five years. Seeing that they'd moved on gave me permission to move on, too.

My trip was already a success.

Living a Life of Purpose

I love facilitating personal-development seminars. I believe that God has given me something special that allows people to trust me with matters of the heart. People share with me the intimate and difficult details of their lives. Even when I was a construction worker, guys often confided in me about private matters.

While I was in Vietnam in 2005, my belief was affirmed that God reveals me to the people who need what I have.

While we were touring one day, I ate the wrong thing and needed to stay close to a restroom. Everyone else toured the Marble Mountains just south of the city of Da Nang. I stayed behind at a small gift-shop area.

I sat on a bench. Two salesclerks sat next to me and started a conversation. Before I knew it, one of the young ladies poured out her heart to me. She said that her dad was an American soldier, but her mom wouldn't tell her anything about her father. She told me about her life of ridicule in school, because of her background. Even her siblings, who are Vietnamese, mocked her.

She was crying. She didn't understand how her dad hadn't looked for her. She went on to say that she usually denies that she is part American, and she couldn't figure out why she was telling me her story.

Our van arrived, and it was time to leave. I was very disturbed that I had to walk away. We went back to the hotel, and I finished the last chapter of the book I was reading—Mitch Albom's *The Five People*

You Meet in Heaven. The message—the exact one I needed to hear to understand the depth of my work—was delivered at just the right time.

I realized that it didn't matter where I was. What I have to offer is visible to those who need it.

I am living a life of purpose. Are you?

The next day, I told our guide that we had to go back to the gift shop before moving on. But the girl was off of work that day. I gave my business card to her friend, and asked our guide to explain that the girl could contact me. He wasn't very open to the whole idea, but I told him to do it, anyway. An hour later, the girl called my cell phone and asked me to come back, but I couldn't.

The entire matter was rather painful.

Our guide gave me the information I needed so I could contact her after I returned to the US. The way I had to leave didn't feel right for me, and I needed some closure. I reached out and eventually located her by phone. We communicated back and forth for a few years. I had the opportunity to help her out by sending her some money when her mother became ill.

I haven't spoken with her in a few years, but she changed my life in a big way. Part of what was stuck inside me was worrying about what we Americans had done during the war. For me, she represented part of the pain that lasted long after the war ended and we left.

Just like for me and everyone else in the war, the effects of the war will never end for her. She will live with being different her whole life.

I now realize that even though I made it home from the war, there isn't a way to "get over" Vietnam. There isn't a way to get over the past.

It's a lifetime journey.

Meeting the Enemy

I t's funny the way life works. When I was in Vietnam during the war, I was blessed. I didn't encounter the enemy. When I returned in 2005, it was different. I actually met the enemy!

Earlier in the book, I shared how I worked for a few days in the Delta. On my return trip, our guide took us back to the Delta for a boat tour. It was really interesting to see how the Vietnamese lived and worked on the river. They actually sell their goods out in the middle of the water! We visited a few small villages that now were tourist attractions.

Around noon, our guide told us that he had a surprise for us: We were going to eat with the enemy! He explained that we would visit a small restaurant owned by a former Viet Cong soldier who was wounded in the war. When we got off our boat in a small cove, I was a little uncomfortable. One of the veterans on our trip was freaked out by the whole ordeal.

The restaurant owner greeted us, and he took us to his restaurant. As our drinks were served, he began a presentation about what he did in the war while fighting against us. He explained how he was wounded by an American mortar and almost died. He lost so much blood that he passed out, but he was rescued. He showed us the scars from his wound, and he talked about how his life eventually got better after the war.

Even though he had done this presentation before, you could tell he was nervous about the whole meeting. Right before we ate lunch together, he said something I will never forget.

"We are not enemies anymore," he said.

I never would've guessed that this visit with an enemy would be so therapeutic, but it was. I saw the look on his face when he said, "We are not enemies anymore." He wasn't sure how we would react.

The veterans on our trip had a mixed set of feelings about the visit, but I could relate to the man. I felt exactly the same way. I wanted to put down the war and my feelings about it, but I wasn't sure that they wanted the same thing. After meeting him, I knew that at least he wanted to put it down. That was good enough for me to move on.

I didn't meet the enemy. I met the *old* enemy!

With each experience on my return trip to Vietnam, the feelings I'd carried inside me for thirty-five years were releasing. I began to understand that the enemy wasn't in Vietnam. The real enemy was in me, and I finally was going to swing open the gate and let him go.

I didn't have to spend the rest of my life on guard duty, trying to keep my feelings locked inside.

Putting It Down

When I returned from Vietnam in 2005, my wife asked what was the biggest thing I learned from going back. I told her that the Vietnam that lived in my head doesn't exist. Nancy said something very interesting to me: "The Vietnam in your head probably never really existed, anyway."

She was right. After thirty-five years of rehashing my memories, I didn't know which details were accurate and which weren't.

What I am clear about is that Vietnam impacted me in a big way and altered the course of my life.

I had a story about Vietnam. At the time, it was a true story. Part of my return trip was to change the story—not to change the facts, but to change my feelings about the story.

Is it time to put down the hurt, fear, or resentment that's been holding you hostage to your past? People hold on to feelings, even if they're painful. Why? They have value. But you must find a new feeling about the event that is more valuable to you than the old feelings. It's the only way to be a leader in your life and in the lives of others.

I now have a fresh view of Vietnam that is more positive and useful than my old memories. I want to share the lessons of my Vietnam experience.

Most of us have our fair share of battles in life. But have you visited the other side of the battlefield? What you call "war" and who you view as the enemy are probably seen differently by those in the battle with you.

How often have you put down the war and opened a dialogue? Maybe it was your war and not theirs. Is it "The Vietnam War" or "The American War"?

It's all about perspective.

We meet the enemy every day—the voice inside your head, the self-criticism and doubt. Are you prisoner to your self-imposed limitations?

On my trip back to Vietnam, I found out that the enemy wasn't there anymore. You may find that the war you've held on to actually ended a long time ago. If you want to move on, you have to forgive. You can't forget, but you can forgive.

If you refuse to forgive, you'll spend a lifetime fighting an internal war.

The only war I could end was the one inside me.

Past, Present, and Future

The three questions that I asked in this book are about the past, present, and future: Am I prepared? Am I safe? Am I alone?

You can't separate your life into compartments like a set of dresser drawers. Try as you may, it's impossible to erase your past. Your past has a big impact on your present life. And your present decisions are the foundation for your future.

Your life will continue to be woven together by past, present, and future events.

Am I prepared? When you ask this question, you review your past experiences and results. If you succeeded in the past, you'll probably feel confident. But if you experienced failure, you may not feel prepared. If you make your current decisions based solely on the past, your future will look just like your past. Because you failed in the past, does that mean you'll fail today or tomorrow?

So am I prepared? I will do my best to keep learning and growing, but I won't know until I finish. I'm prepared to make new decisions each day. I'm prepared to make mistakes along the way. I'm prepared to surround myself with the best people. I'm prepared to make unpopular choices that I think are the right decisions. I'm prepared to make it up when I don't feel prepared. I'm prepared to have fun with all my decisions and with the people I interact with each day. I'm prepared to die someday and know that I lived a full life.

Am I safe? Fear is the biggest hindrance to living a great life. Most people experience fear from two perspectives. The first source of fear is past experiences where the outcome is perceived as bad. The second source of fear is the unknown. It's easy to understand the struggle: You can't change the past or guarantee the future, so making decisions in the present is scary. What role does fear play as you make decisions and take action—or not take action?

So am I safe? I'm often afraid as I face tough decisions, but this doesn't mean that I'm not safe. Sometimes I feel like I'm walking point in Vietnam again. But even when I don't feel safe, I can act anyway. Fear is just a feeling. It's what I do with that fear that matters.

Am I alone? Feeling alone is common. Maybe it's not your parents' fault that you feel alone—or your boss's or your ex-wife's or your old high-school flame's. Could it be that feeling alone is just a feeling all of us have? How is feeling alone any different than any of the other fears you have?

So am I alone? I have a great circle of influence, but I often do feel as if I'm alone. I wish I could take a break from leadership sometimes, but it doesn't work that way. Being alone is not being lonely. When the buck stops with me, alone is good. It's my decision.

All three questions usually are evoked by emotions, and the bottom-line emotion is the feeling of fear. If you took feelings out of the equation and did a logical checklist, your results would change dramatically.

If you want to accomplish something different—if you want to be a leader—the three questions change to something like this:

- Do I want to do this? Yes or no.
- Has someone else done it? Yes or no.
- Do I need help? Yes or no.

And this is the action step: Just do it!

Once you pull the drama out of your decision making, the pace immediately picks up. Feelings—especially the feeling of fear—are the reasons most people use to slow down life. Why do you slow down your life? So you can feel as if you're in control and minimize your fear of failure or of being hurt?

Don't get lost in your past experiences or your fear of the future. The only way I know that you can master your present is to stay in it.

It's a Wonderful Life

Life is a journey of fighting for freedom. At least, that's been my journey. And now my journey is about teaching others how to find their way to freedom, how to lead.

Empowering people to find the answers that are right for them is what my work—my life—is all about.

Each person decides what freedom means for him or her. If you don't fight for what's important to you, you're leaving your life to chance.

We all face the challenges that life delivers. We're all walking point and feeling the pressure of leading our families, careers, and communities. That pressure can create self-doubt and the belief that your life has little meaning.

My life became a wonderful life when I decided that I was going to change and move forward in a different way.

When I decided that I was going to change, my past began to change. I realized that everything I had done and experienced was the foundation for my future. I originally thought that my past was a collection of problems and bad choices. When I decided to change, my perspective of my past changed. I was doing the best I could with the tools I knew how to use.

Now I was prepared to retool and find new applications so I could meet my needs in a healthier way.

I'm a common man, but I'm also a special man. I know that I'm loved by a lot of people and have already made a bigger difference in life than I ever could've imagined. My life changed when I committed to being the best man I could be.

I embrace the fact that I am blessed.

What about you? Are you ready to answer the important questions in your life? My hope is that this book has sparked something inside of you so you live a wonderful life.

If you've thought that you're common and that your life isn't special, you're mistaken. It doesn't matter how you were raised or whether you felt like you were loved or not. It doesn't matter if you're rich or poor. It doesn't matter how much education you have or whether you excelled or failed in school.

If you struggle with past failures, you can do something different today. If you've been afraid that life won't work out in the future, you can do something different today.

It's your decision.

You have a choice to act, regardless of your feelings. The world can't answer your questions. You decide the answers in your own life.

What matters is that you realize that you're special and important. There's never been—and never will be—another person as unique as you. Think about how life would be different if you'd never lived.

When you understand that your life is a gift to the world, you'll find more purpose in your interactions with the people in your circle. Each day that you live a life of purpose, you'll feel a sense of gratitude and realize that you're truly blessed. You really will be a leader, twenty-four hours a day.

Once you realize that you're blessed, it won't matter what happens. Why? *It's all a blessing.*

And the whole world will know that you are the star in your own wonderful life!

"All you can take with you is that which you've given away."

—It's a Wonderful Life

Acknowledgments

First and foremost, thank you to my wife, Nancy, who has believed in me and supported my crazy ideas. Thanks for listening when I needed you and for giving me the freedom to go out and continue to risk, even after some failures.

My five grown children and their spouses—Brian and Megan, Julie and Rob, Coleen and Justin, Brad, and Russ—have sacrificed family time to allow me to do what I love. Thank you.

And thanks to the future of our family, my four grandchildren: Emma, Michael, Zach, and Ella.

Thank you to all of my teachers for the gift of difficult learning, including:

- Sister Mary Lucille, who failed me in the third grade and changed the course of my life. While that event challenges me to this day, it also inspired me to find a way to simplify life and help others connect the dots.
- Jim Quinn, who was my inspiration to become a facilitator with Life Success Seminars.
- Steve Sherwood, who taught me the magic of opening people to their dreams.
- Dan Rolfes, my mentor, who encourages me to take big risks and dream big dreams.

Thank you to Tony Miller and Sam Wilder for helping me think outside the box.

Special thanks goes to Ann Weber, my editor extraordinaire and friend. Ann came to my rescue and got me moving when I had writer's block. She's been in my corner ever since.

Thank you to Mike Mitzel for all of his work, including the book-cover design.

Thank you to Ken Williamson for his encouragement and planning our return trip to Vietnam in 2005.

Thanks to all of my supporters who believed in me and in this book. Special thanks goes to Tim and Peg Mathile, Thane Maynard, and Matthew Kelly.

And thank you to the graduates of Life Success Seminars. Your support made this book release such an exciting adventure!